LANDMARKS OF
THE CIVIL WAR

American Landmarks

JAMES OLIVER HORTON
General Editor

LANDMARKS OF
THE CIVIL WAR

Nina Silber

OXFORD
UNIVERSITY PRESS

Published in association with the
National Register of Historic Places, National Park Service, the National Parks Foundation
and Gilder Lehrman Institute of American History

OXFORD
UNIVERSITY PRESS

Oxford   New York
Auckland   Bangkok   Buenos Aires   Cape Town   Chennai
Dar es Salaam   Delhi   Hong Kong   Istanbul   Karachi   Kolkata
Kuala Lumpur   Madrid   Melbourne   Mexico City   Mumbai   Nairobi
São Paulo   Shanghai   Singapore   Taipei   Tokyo   Toronto

Published by Oxford University Press, Inc.
198 Madison Avenue, New York, New York, 10016
www.oup.com

Oxford is a registered trademark of Oxford University Press

Library of Congress Cataloging-in-Publication Data

Silber, Nina.
   Landmarks of the Civil War / Nina Silber.
      p. cm. — (American landmarks)
"Published in association with the National Register of Historic Places,
National Park Service, and the National Parks Foundation."
Includes bibliographical references (p.) and index.
   ISBN 0-19-512920-2 (alk. paper)
1. Historic sites—United States. 2. United States—History—Civil War,
1861–1865—Battlefields. 3. United States—History—Civil War,
1861–1865—Monuments. 4. United States—History, Local.
I. National Register of Historic Places. II. National Parks Foundation (U.S.)
III. Title. IV. American landmarks (Oxford University Press)
   E159 .S58 2003
   973.7—dc21   2002014896

Printing number: 9 8 7 6 5 4 3 2 1

Printed in Hong Kong
on acid-free paper

Cover: *Antietam National Battlefield is the site of the Battle of Antietam on September 17, 1862. It was the bloodiest single day of the Civil War and cost more than twenty-three thousand casualties. The rolling terrain benefitted artillerists of both armies, allowing them to fire their cannons effectively and strike enemy troop positions at great distances. The New York State Monument (in the background) commemorates the services of its officers and soldiers in the battle.*

Frontispiece: *On February 18, 1861, Jefferson Davis (standing at the doorway between the center columns) was inaugurated at the Alabama State Capitol as the first and only President of the Confederate States of America. The event marked the formal beginning of the Confederacy, which for the next four years would wage a brutal civil war with the Union*

Titlepage: *Soldiers at a Signal Station at Elk Mountain, Antietam, Md.*

American Landmarks

JAMES OLIVER HORTON
General Editor

Landmarks of African-American History

Landmarks of American Immigration

Landmarks of American Indian History

Landmarks of American Literature

Landmarks of the American Presidents

Landmarks of American Religion

Landmarks of the American Revolution

Landmarks of American Science & Invention

Landmarks of American Sports

Landmarks of American Women's History

Landmarks of the Civil War

Landmarks of Liberty

Landmarks of the Old South

LANDMARKS OF
The Civil War

Contents

INTRODUCTION 8

HOW TO USE THIS BOOK 10

PREFACE 12

1 THE COOPER UNION BUILDING
The Site of Lincoln's Speech on Slavery 14

2 FORT SUMTER NATIONAL MONUMENT
The First Military Engagement 25

3 THE WHITE HOUSE OF THE CONFEDERACY
The South's Social and Political Center 34

4 MANASSAS NATIONAL BATTLEFIELD PARK
A Battleground for Soldiers and Journalists..................46

5 NATIONAL MUSEUM OF AMERICAN ART AND
NATIONAL PORTRAIT GALLERY
A Hospital for the Wounded Soldiers..........................56

6 TANNEHILL FURNACE
A Foundry for the Tools of War 63

7 PORT HUDSON
A Sacred Ground for Emancipation 71

8 GETTYSBURG NATIONAL MILITARY PARK
The War at a Turning Point 83

9 HONEY SPRINGS BATTLEFIELD
A Native American Battleground 96

10 ANDERSONVILLE NATIONAL HISTORIC SITE
A Prison Site of the Confederacy 106

11 APPOMATTOX COURT HOUSE NATIONAL
HISTORICAL PARK
A Place of Surrender...115

12 ARLINGTON HOUSE,
THE ROBERT E. LEE MEMORIAL
A Final Resting Place for the Civil War Dead 124

CHRONOLOGY 132

FURTHER READING 134

INDEX 137

PAGE 14
The Cooper Union Building

PAGE 46
Manassas National Battlefield Park

PAGE 90
Gateway to Gettysburg Cemetery

Introduction:
The Power of Place

James Oliver Horton

General Editor

Few experiences can connect us with our past more completely than walking the ground where our history happened. The landmarks of American history have a vital role to play in helping us to understand our past, because they are its physical evidence. The sensory experience of a place can help us to reconstruct historical events, just as archaeologists reconstruct vanished civilizations. It can also inspire us to empathy with those who came before us. A place can take hold of us, body, mind, and spirit. As philosophers of the Crow Indian nation have reminded us, "The ground on which we stand is sacred ground. It is the blood of our ancestors." It is the history owed to our children. They will remember that history only to the extent that we preserve the places where it was made.

Historical sites are some of history's best teachers. In the early 1970s, when I was a graduate student in Boston, working on a study of the nineteenth-century black community of that city, I walked the streets of Beacon Hill imagining the daily lives of those who lived there a century before. Although I had learned much about the people of that community from their newspapers and pamphlets, from their personal letters and official records, nothing put me in touch with their lives and their time like standing in the places where they had stood and exploring the neighborhood where they lived.

I remember walking along Myrtle Street just down Beacon Hill from the rear of the Massachusetts State House in the early morning and realizing that Leonard Grimes, the black minister of the Fugitive Slave Church, must have squinted into the sun just as I was doing as he emerged from his home at the rear of number 59 and turned left on his way to his church. Walking up Joy Street in December added new meaning to descriptions I had read about the sound of children sledding down its slope during the particularly snowy winter of 1850. And twisting my ankle on irregular cobblestone streets made clear the precarious footing for fugitive slaves fleeing at full run from slave catchers empowered by the Fugitive Slave Law of 1850.

Any historical event is much better understood within the context of its historical setting. It is one thing to read the details of the Battle of Gettysburg. It is quite another to stand on Little Round Top, with its commanding view of the battlefield to the north and west, and contemplate the assault of the Fifteenth Alabama Confederates against the downhill charge of the Twentieth Maine Volunteer Infantry. Standing at the summit, taking the measure of the degree of slope and the open area that afforded little cover to advancing armies is an unforgettable experience. It also bears irrefutable testimony to the horror of that battle, the bloodiest of the Civil War, and to the sacrifice of the more than fifty thousand men during four days in the summer of 1863.

The Landmarks of American History series has emerged from this belief in the power of place to move us and to teach us. It was with this same philosophy in mind that in 1966 Congress authorized the establishment of the National Register of Historic Places, "the Nation's official list of cultural resources worthy of preservation." These enduring symbols of the American experience are as diverse as the immigration station on Angel Island in San Francisco Bay, which served as U.S. entry point for thousands of Asian immigrants; or Sinclair Lewis's Boyhood Home in Sauk Centre, Minnesota, the place that inspired the novelist's Nobel Prize-winning descriptions of small-town America; or the Cape Canaveral Air Force Station in Florida, launch site of Neil Armstrong's historic trip to the moon. Taken together, such places define us as a nation.

The historic sites presented in this series are selected from the National Register, and they are more than interesting places. The books in this series are written by some of our finest historians—based at universities, historic museums, and historic sites—all nationally recognized experts on the central themes of their respective volumes. For them, historic sites are not just places to visit on a field trip, but primary sources that inform their scholarship. Not simply illustrations of history, they bring the reality of our past to life, making it meaningful to our present and useful for our future.

How to Use This Book

This book is designed to tell the story of American history from a unique perspective: the places where it was made. Each chapter profiles a historic site listed on the National Register of Historic Places, and each site is used as the centerpiece for discussion of a particular aspect of history—for example, Independence Hall for the Declaration of Independence, or the Woolworth store in the Downtown Greensboro Historic District for Martin Luther King Jr.'s role in the civil rights movement. This book is not intended as an architectural history; it is an American history.

On page 6 (opposite the table of contents), there is a regional map of the United States locating each of the main sites covered in this volume. Each chapter in this volume contains a main essay that explains the site's historical importance; a fact box (explained below); and one or two maps that locate the site in the region or show its main features. Each chapter also contains a box listing sites related to the main subject. For each related site, the box includes the official name, address, phone, website, whether it is a National Historic Landmark (NHL) or part of the National Park Service (NPS), and a short description. As much as possible, the author has selected related sites that are geographically diverse and open to the public.

Many of the chapters feature primary sources related to the thematic discussion. These include, for example, letters, journal entries, legal documents, and newspaper articles. Each primary source is introduced by an explanatory note or a caption, indicated by the symbol ♣.

At the back of the book is a timeline of important events mentioned in the text, along with a few other major events that help give a chronological context for the book's theme. A list of further reading includes site-specific reading, along with general reading pertinent to the book.

Fact Boxes

Each chapter has a fact box containing reference information for its main site. This box includes a picture of the site; the site's official name on the National Register;

contact information; National Register Information System number (which you can you use to obtain more details about the site from the National Register, whose contact information appears at the back of this book); whether the site is a National Historic Landmark (NHL) or part of the National Park Service (NPS); and important dates, people, and events in the site's history.

Acts of Congress recognize and protect America's 386 National Park Service units, including National Parks, National Historic Sites, National Historic Battlefields, and National Monuments. The Secretary of the Interior designates National Historic Landmarks, of which there are more than 2,300. States, federal agencies, and Indian tribes have nominated the majority of the seventy-five thousand properties listed in the National Register of Historic Places, some of which are also historic units of the National Park Service and National Historic Landmarks.

Picture of site ────────

Official site name ────────

Valley Forge National Historic Park

Contact information ──────── Valley Forge, PA 19482
610-783-1077

Website ──────── *www.nps.gov/vafo*

National Register Information System number NRIS 66000657

Site is a National Historic Landmark/ NHL/NPS
National Park Service owns or maintains site

Date built or other significant dates ────────

DATE OF ENCAMPMENT
Winter 1777–78

Architect, builder, or original owner ────────

ORIGINAL OWNER
Laetitia Penn, daughter of Pennsylvania's founder, William Penn

SIGNIFICANCE
Summary of site's significance ──────── At Valley Forge Washington's army struggled to keep warm, overcame a poorly organized supply system, and summoned up the discipline and courage to renew fighting when spring arrived. The winter encampment became a test of the army's ability to survive, and therefore a test of the nation's as well.

Preface

The Civil War may well have been the most pivotal event in American history. It maintained and then reshaped the United States as a nation; it set in motion the liberation of 4 million slaves; and it irrevocably changed the lives of millions of Americans who participated in, or simply endured, the four years of conflict. It also left an indelible stamp on the American landscape: the war saw both the destruction of homes and factories and bridges, and the creation of new workshops and new avenues of transportation. Most notably, the Civil War transformed sites of peacetime habitation into scenes of struggle. It transformed tranquil wheatfields and peaceful forests into scenes of terrifying slaughter. It changed opulent buildings and simple churches into overcrowded hospitals. And in one of the most remarkable alterations, the Civil War remade a magnificent Southern plantation into the burial ground for thousands of dead soldiers.

Without question, it is the battlefields that dominate our images of the Civil War landscape. We see them today, crowded in sections of Virginia and Maryland, in Pennsylvania, in parts of Louisiana and Mississippi, returned once again to scenes of peace, yet preserved so that generations of Americans will remember the bloody moments of war. This book calls attention to some but by no means all of the critical battlefields that were the sites of important events in the history of the war. Its aim is to show the types of places where the war occurred, not just the military conflict, but the all-consuming experience that affected millions of Americans—white and black, men and women—in countless ways.

In this regard, I have tried to give a sense of the wide variety of ways in which Americans became enmeshed in the war, and so have chosen twelve landmarks that reflect the broad scope of Civil War activities. The approach of the book is thematic, and the themes explored are both military and civilian.

In some cases, I have looked at battlefields as the scenes where significant contributions were made by different groups of Americans: African Americans, who fought on the high bluffs of the Mississippi River at Port Hudson, Louisiana; Native Americans, who fought on the Oklahoma plains near Honey Springs; and journalists, who got their baptism in war reporting at the battle site of Bull Run.

In other cases, I have tried to illuminate aspects of the war, which occurred outside the battlefields: the soldiers' experience of captivity in some of the war's notorious prison sites; the hospital experience in the often inadequate and makeshift medical quarters; the technical side of war in workshops that churned out weapons and ammunition; and the politics of war-making in official Presidential and legislative settings.

I have also examined three sites which roughly mark the beginning, middle, and end points of the war—Fort Sumter, Gettysburg, and Appomattox—as a way to understand the progress of the conflict at some of its most critical junctures.

In order to understand the onset of the Civil War, I have begun with New York's Cooper Union, the scene of a key speech by Abraham Lincoln which ultimately helped secure his nomination as the Republican Presidential candidate in 1860. At the end, in order to understand something about the human price that was paid, I have examined Robert E. Lee's estate at Arlington that was transformed during the war into an enormous burial ground.

The Civil War was fought in many ways, and in far more places than can be contained in a single volume. I hope that this book will introduce readers to the variety of ways in which the war affected the American people. I hope that it will show how the war marked a decisive moment in transforming the places where Americans lived, worked, farmed, and did business. Perhaps, too, this volume can tell us something about why many of these Civil War landmarks continue to have such a symbolic hold on the American imagination.

The Cooper Union Building

New York, N.Y.

The Site of Lincoln's Speech on Slavery

Before delivering his speech at Cooper Union (below), Abraham Lincoln visited photographer Mathew Brady's New York studio to have his portrait done (above). He appeared without his characteristic facial hair, not having a beard until the following year. The Cooper Union Building, home to the Great Hall, stood as an impressive landmark in New York City.

As Abraham Lincoln prepared the speech he would deliver in New York City's Cooper Union Building in February 1860, he was certainly aware of an ever-widening political rift that threatened to divide the United States in two. Blood had already been shed in Kansas, where proslavery and antislavery settlers had battled each other for political control of the territory. Supporters of slavery had recently been cheered by the Supreme Court's Dred Scott decision.

Scott, a Missouri slave, had demanded his freedom due to his extended residence in free territory, where his slaveowner had taken him. The Supreme Court ruled against him. This decision denied Scott his freedom. It also opened the possibility for the unlimited spread of slavery through Utah, New Mexico, and other new Western territories.

In reaction to the Supreme Court decision, a new political party—the Republicans—had formed. The party was committed to reversing the Dred Scott decision and ending the westward expansion of slavery. Some had taken even stronger steps against the South's "peculiar institution," as many Southern whites called it.

In the fall of 1859, the abolitionist John Brown had led a raid against the federal arsenal in then Harpers Ferry, Virginia, hoping to encourage

slaves to rebel and join abolitionists against the slave system. The raid had ended in failure and Brown had been executed just two months before Lincoln's appearance in New York.

Lincoln arrived in New York as Americans began to speculate about the upcoming presidential election in November and who the new Republican party would choose as its candidate. William Seward, a noted statesman and senator from New York, was considered by many as the most likely choice because of his forceful statements against the spread of slavery. But others in the party favored a midwestern candidate, believing that the party needed to secure stronger support from midwestern states, such as Indiana and Illinois, in order to do well.

Abraham Lincoln, although perceived as not particularly presidential, had, nonetheless, attracted attention during his recent unsuccessful bid for the Illinois Senate seat. The series of debates between Lincoln and the incumbent Illinois senator, Democrat Stephen Douglas, had drawn attention to Lincoln's reasoned and moderate positions that supported Republican ideals.

A seasoned lawyer from Springfield, Illinois, Lincoln often belittled his own preparedness for the Presidency. At the same time, he took concrete steps to advance his candidacy. He was especially pleased at the opportunity to present himself before an East Coast audience and accepted an invitation to speak before the congregation of Reverend Henry Ward Beecher's Brooklyn church in February 1860.

Astute New York Republicans quickly recognized that a larger, more central location would offer a better venue for Lincoln's speech than a relatively remote house of worship. Several saw political possibilities in this upcoming lecture, especially those who preferred to see someone other than Seward receive the party's nomination. Under the sponsorship of the Young Men's Central Republican Union, Lincoln's New York speech was set for February 27, and the site was moved from Beecher's church to the Cooper Union Building (commonly referred to as Cooper Union) at Manhattan's Astor Place.

If the goal of the speech was to attract political visibility for the relatively unknown Abraham Lincoln, then Cooper Union was the most logical venue. The Cooper Union had been founded just the year prior to Lincoln's

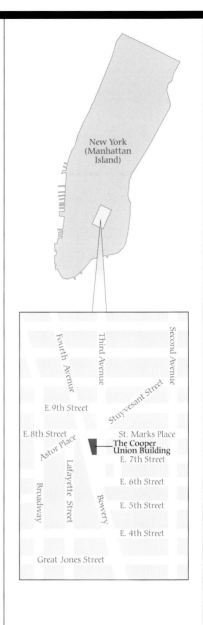

Industrialist, inventor, and social reformer, Peter Cooper founded the school that bore his name in 1859. His inventions and innovations—including iron beams and a circular elevator shaft—made the Cooper Union Building ahead of its time.

visit by Peter Cooper, an extremely successful industrialist and inventor. Feeling burdened by his lack of formal schooling, Cooper was determined to provide less well-to-do New Yorkers with an institution that would offer an advanced education at no cost, using the fortunes he made in his glue business and his iron foundry. Like other wealthy New Yorkers, Cooper was alarmed at signs of social strife between the city's rich and the poor and hoped to relieve some of the social tension with the new establishment.

During the 1850s, Cooper laid the foundation for the institution that would bear his name. In fact, he literally helped lay the foundation by participating in the cornerstone-laying ceremony in 1853. The school, known as The Cooper Union for the Advancement of Science and Art, opened in 1859 and offered free education for men and women in engineering and architectural drawing. It soon became a site not only for classroom study but also for important public lectures.

Frederick A. Peterson, a Prussian architect, designed the five-story brick and brownstone building. Its Italianate style was marked in particular by loggias—ornate covered balconies—on the north and south ends. The building also bore the marks of Peter Cooper's innovative, industrial career and, in this regard, stands as a symbol of the developing industrial capacity of the Northern states in the years before the Civil War.

The most notable innovation in the building's construction was the use of a new type of beam, made of wrought iron in Cooper's own iron works in Trenton, New Jersey. Only a few buildings had used this method, prior to the construction of the Cooper Union Building. Nearly all other buildings of the time relied either on stone, which was heavy and costly, or wood, which could catch fire. In contrast, wrought iron had greater strength and was also inflammable.

The Cooper Union Building, built with iron beams twenty feet long, represented a structural innovation and, in effect, anticipated the skyscrapers of the twentieth century. A more curious feature of the building was a circular shaft that Cooper had installed, anticipating a time when elevators, used only rarely in the 1850s, would become more widespread.

The first two floors of the building originally housed shops and offices, whose rents were used to help finance the school. The basement contained Cooper Union's huge lecture hall, known as the Great Hall, in which New Yorkers could receive further edification on the political and cultural currents of the day. In February 1860, the nine-hundred-seat hall was the largest lecture facility in New York and would offer the aspiring Lincoln a grand and expanded format for his pronouncements. Indeed, despite a driving snowstorm on the night of his speech, Cooper Union's Great Hall was filled to capacity.

Many who braved the snow that February night may have expected the speaker to be a rude hayseed from the far-off frontier. As one observer recalled, Lincoln struck a "long, ungainly figure, upon which hung clothes that, while new for the trip, were evidently the work of an unskilled tailor." This same observer went on to describe Lincoln's "long, gaunt head capped by a shock of hair that seemed not to have been thoroughly brushed out." Then, when the unkempt midwesterner began his speech, his voice sounded unusually high, even piercing. In short, he "made a picture which did not fit in with New York's conception of a finished statesman."

However, the speech turned out to be an awe-inspiring performance and one of the most important Lincoln would make. He began by emphasizing the power of the federal government —as established by the United States Constitution—to exclude slavery from the new territories. This issue of slavery in the new territories had emerged as one of the most critical issues of the 1850s, especially since the nation had been rapidly expanding and acquiring new territory, which included a huge expanse of land won from Mexico during the Mexican war.

The distinctive engineering and architectural attributes of the Cooper Union Building drew the attention of Scientific American *which depicted the impressive edifice in an 1885 illustration.*

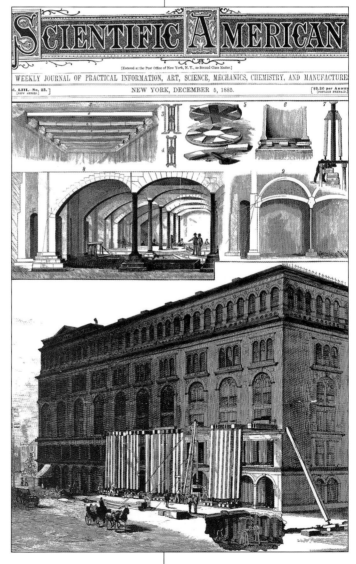

The Cooper Union Building

Cooper Square
7th Street and 4th Avenue
New York, NY 10003
212-353-4169
www.cooper.edu

NRIS 66000540
NHL

DATE BUILT
1853–59

ARCHITECT
Frederick A. Peterson

SIGNIFICANCE
The building is the site of a
critical 1860 speech by Abraham
Lincoln on the subject of slavery
and national expansion.

Southern slaveowners had adopted a fairly aggressive position in asserting their right to bring slaves to the new territories. The Republicans and the Northerners, who rallied around the newly formed Republican party, came to look upon this prospect with increasing alarm.

Although they had moral objections to human bondage, many white Northerners, more significantly, had come to look upon slavery as a threat to their own livelihoods. They saw slaves as unfair competition for the individual laborers trying to earn decent wages or settle and work their own farms independently. Moreover, these Northerners argued, slavery hampered the overall economic and industrial progress of the nation.

This part of the argument would have been well-known to Lincoln's listeners in New York. So, in his Cooper Union speech, Lincoln was less concerned with elaborating on his stand against slavery and more concerned with explaining the errors of those who did not come out forcefully against Southerner's aims to expand slavery—especially his long-time rival Stephen Douglas.

Lincoln attacked Douglas's position which denied the federal government's right to control slavery in the territories. He also opposed Douglas's proposal to allow settlers in the new territories to vote on slavery themselves, a measure referred to as "popular sovereignty."

By carefully reviewing the historical records and the accounts of the 1789 constitutional convention, Lincoln offered concrete evidence that the majority of the nation's founders believed in the power of the federal government to oversee, and even exclude, slavery in the territories. In this way, Lincoln drew a straight line from the hallowed words of the founding fathers to the principles of his party and their supporters. In short, Lincoln demonstrated that the Republicans were the true heirs of the Republican tradition, upon which the nation had been founded.

Lincoln also made it clear that slavery was an immoral institution. This Republican view of slavery as inherently evil placed the party in direct opposition to Southern slaveowners. Indeed, Lincoln warned, Southerners' insistence on the benefits of slavery would soon lead them to press for "the nationalization of bondage"—a dire threat to freedom-loving Northerners. Lincoln ended his argument with a forceful, dramatic conclusion. "Let us have faith," he intoned in one of his most well-known proclamations, "that right makes might, and in that faith, let us, to the end, dare to do our duty as we understand it." His final words brought the audience to their feet, applauding and loudly cheering their approval of his stand. Lincoln, said one reporter on the scene, is "the greatest man since St. Paul."

Word spread rapidly that Abraham Lincoln had eloquently and impressively upheld the Republican principles opposing the expansion of slavery. As he traveled through New England following his New York appearance to visit his son Robert, who was studying at Harvard, Lincoln found himself in great demand at political rallies and events. Perhaps most importantly, the Cooper Union speech brought Lincoln attention from the leaders of the Republican party, who now viewed him as an extremely viable presidential candidate.

Several Republican newspapers issued pamphlet editions of the speech, making it widely available as a triumphant statement of the party's outlook. By the time he returned home to Illinois, Abraham Lincoln was several steps closer to becoming a candidate, in large part due to the success of the Cooper Union speech. By May, he had become the official Republican nominee, and by November, he had secured his place as the sixteenth president of the United States. That victory, however, began the process which ultimately culminated in the secession of eleven Southern states from the Union and the beginning of the Civil War.

Cooper Union continued in its educational mission during the Civil War and the building became a pivotal spot for political rallies and organizing, especially for Northern women. On April 26, 1861, with the Civil War only two weeks old, the Great Hall became the scene of a huge meeting of ladies, who came together to create a central organization that could coordinate women's relief efforts throughout the course of the war. The organization, called the

Before the Civil War, increasing numbers of Americans came to oppose the forced bondage of African Americans in the South. These slaves belonged to T. F. Drayton of Hilton Head, South Carolina.

What Caused the Civil War?

For years since the time of the conflict, historians have debated the question of what caused Americans to fight against one another in the Civil War. Students of history have considered a variety of factors, including constitutional issues and economic differences. However until fairly recently, many have sidestepped the most obvious factor that led to the war: slavery.

When the war ended, Confederates and their supporters argued that the South had gone to war not to protect its "peculiar institution" but to defend its constitutional principles. According to this argument, Southerners believed firmly in the principles of states' rights and limited federal power, and objected to the Republican government's attempt to dictate to the Southern states.

While Northerners were somewhat more inclined to see slavery as a factor in causing the war, historians often tried to minimize the importance of slavery, viewing it as one of many economic factors that divided the North from the South. Indeed, a popular interpretation in the twentieth century argued that Northerners fought to promote industrial capitalist growth, while Southerners fought to preserve an agrarian way of life. This argument maintained that Northerners felt just as strongly about high tariffs and an expanded system of internal improvements as they did about slavery.

In the middle years of the twentieth century, a revisionist interpretation emerged regarding the causes of the Civil War, an interpretation that differed from an earlier view, which argued that the war was inevitable. The revisionists maintained that, far from being inevitable, the war was caused by unscrupulous politicians, who built their political careers on the slavery issue. These historians suggested that slavery was on the road to extinction but that politicians—with both Northern and Southern lawmakers taking various amounts of the blame—prodded their constituents into a hostile state of mind by focusing on slavery.

Today, most historians agree that slavery and the increasingly heated conflict over the expansion of slavery into the Western territories were the decisive factors in causing the Civil War. Most agree, too, that the Confederates were, first and foremost, committed to slavery and only secondarily to states' rights as a way to block federal interference with its system of bondage.

Many argue as well that Northerners opposed slavery not because they were committed to a program of industrial growth, but because they were committed to "free labor," the idea that individuals must be free to control their own ability to work, and thereby, better their circumstances. Although there is some disagreement among historians as to what lay behind the voters' political views, many agree that a growing body of Northerners came to view the expansion of slavery as a threat to their ambitions to own land and advance themselves economically.

Some Northerners agreed with Lincoln's argument in the Cooper Union speech that slavery was morally wrong. A larger portion, although not condemning slavery on moral grounds, agreed with Lincoln that the expansion of slavery would have detrimental effects on the health and prosperity of the American nation.

Woman's Central Association of Relief (WCAR), helped to form an extensive network of the women's volunteer support groups that had begun to spring up everywhere in the Northeast. It served as the headquarters for many women on the home front, who immediately turned their attention to various tasks such as sewing shirts, knitting socks, preparing bandages, and packaging food for the soldiers who had departed for the war from their towns and villages. It also recruited nurses, who could attend to the sick and wounded soldiers, and work to provide supplies to meet the Union Army's needs and wants.

The WCAR was a forerunner of the United States Sanitary Commission, an umbrella organization run primarily by prominent men, which coordinated volunteer societies throughout the Northern states. When it was established, the WCAR became one of the main branches of the Sanitary Commission and gave women new positions of authority and leadership during the Civil War.

Shortly after the April meeting in the Great Hall, the WCAR opened an office in the Cooper Union Building. It became a central depot for great quantities of army supplies, as well as a clearing house of information for women, who wished to know how best to supply the

In April 1861, soon after the Civil War began, Northern women met in Cooper Union's Great Hall to organize the Woman's Central Association of Relief. The WCAR, which sent medical supplies to soldiers and recruited nurses, attracted numerous women who strongly felt the need to contribute to the war effort.

Lincoln's Stirring Words in the Great Hall

 Abraham Lincoln astonished New Yorkers with the speech he delivered to a packed Great Hall at Cooper Union on February 27, 1860. Nine months later, he was elected the sixteenth President of the United States. He concluded his stirring speech with these remarks on the need to fight slavery.

A few words now to Republicans. It is exceedingly desirable that all parts of this great Confederacy shall be at peace, and in harmony with one another. Let us Republicans do our part to have it so. Even though much provoked, let us do nothing through passion and ill temper. . . . Judging by all they say and do, and by the subject and nature of their controversy with us, let us determine, if we can, what will satisfy them.

Will they be satisfied if the Territories be unconditionally surrendered to them? We know they will not. In all their present complaints against us, the Territories are scarcely mentioned. Invasions and insurrections are the rage now. Will it satisfy them if, in the future, we have nothing to do with invasions and insurrections? We know it will not. We so know, because we know we never had anything to do with invasions and insurrections; and yet this total abstaining does not exempt us from the charge and the denunciation. . . . Holding, as they do, that slavery is morally right and socially elevating, they cannot cease to demand a full national recognition of it as a legal right and a social blessing.

Nor can we justifiably withhold this on any ground save our conviction that slavery is wrong. If slavery is right, all words, acts, laws, and constitutions against it are themselves wrong, and should be silenced and swept away. If it is right, we cannot justly object to its nationality—its universality; if it is wrong, they cannot justly insist upon its extension—its enlargement. All they ask we could readily grant, if we thought slavery right; all we ask they could as readily grant, if they thought it wrong. Their thinking it right and our thinking it wrong is the precise fact upon which depends the whole controversy. Thinking it right, as they do, they are not to blame for desiring its full recognition as being right; but thinking it wrong, as we do, can we yield to them? Can we cast our votes with their view, and against our own? In view of our moral, social, and political responsibilities, can we do this?

Wrong as we think slavery is, we can yet afford to let it alone where it is, because that much is due to the necessity arising from its actual presence in the nation; but can we, while our votes will prevent it, allow it to spread into the national Territories, and to overrun us here in these free States? If our sense of duty forbids this, then let us stand by our duty fearlessly and effectively. . . .

Neither let us be slandered from our duty by false accusations against us, nor frightened from it by menaces of destruction to the government, nor of dungeons to ourselves. Let us have faith that right makes might, and in that faith let us to the end dare to do our duty as we understand it.

army's needs. For example, New York women could visit the Cooper Union office to get sewing instructions for some of the garments the soldiers required. One woman wrote to her sister early in the war that she was "going to the Cooper Union today to try and get some simple patterns for calico gowns. They advertise to supply paper patterns of garments to ladies."

The office stayed open for the duration of the war, even during the violent New York City draft riots in 1863, which were partly caused by unequal conscription laws that allowed those who could afford it to pay to avoid military service. The WCAR headquarters closed several months after the war's conclusion in April 1865.

After the war, Cooper Union remained an important gathering place and educational facility for New Yorkers. Remodeled in the 1880s and 1890s, and then thoroughly overhauled in the 1970s, Cooper Union continues today as the only private, full-scholarship college which focuses its exclusive attention on preparing students in architecture, art, and engineering.

At the beginning of the twentieth century, conservators and architects undertook an ambitious plan to restore the building's exterior. Throughout the decades of education and renovation, the Great Hall has hosted an impressive pageant of American speakers: from women suffragists to NAACP organizers, and from Theodore Roosevelt to William Jefferson Clinton. New York's Cooper Union has offered a platform for reformers and politicians and has provided a vital arena for public conversation.

After it was initiated in the Great Hall in April 1861, the Woman's Central Association of Relief (WCAR) occupied an office in one of the storefronts in the Cooper Union Building. Here, WCAR volunteers packed boxes of supplies to send to troops and distributed materials to women, who wished to make clothes and other items for soldiers.

The Lincoln family lived in this home in Springfield, Illinois, when Abraham Lincoln won the presidential contest of 1861.

LINCOLN MEMORIAL

National Mall
Washington, DC 20004
202-426-6841
www.nps.gov/linc
NPS

In the generations after the Civil War, Abraham Lincoln achieved a near-mythic status for his role in the war. This prompted public officials to construct a grandiose memorial to him, more than seventy years after his death. Built in 1938 and modeled after a Greek temple with white marble columns, this monument contains a statue of President Lincoln by the sculptor Daniel Chester French. The walls of the monument are carved with the texts of two of Lincoln's famous speeches, the Gettysburg Address and his Second Inaugural Address.

LINCOLN HOME NATIONAL HISTORIC SITE

426 South Seventh Street
(Visitors Center)
Springfield, IL 62701
217-523-0222
www.nps.gov/liho
NHL/NPS

Lincoln and his family lived in this house between 1844 and 1861, when Lincoln was a prominent Springfield attorney. This is the only house Lincoln ever owned. While living in this house, he was elected to U.S. Congress, and later, to the presidency of the United States. The historic site encompasses the surrounding neighborhood.

FORD'S THEATER NATIONAL HISTORIC SITE

511 10th Street NW
Washington, DC 20004
202-426-6924
www.nps.gov/foth
NPS

While attending a theatrical production in this building, Abraham Lincoln was assassinated by John Wilkes Booth, a Confederate sympathizer, on April 14, 1865—five days after Robert E. Lee surrendered to Ulysses S. Grant at Appomattox Court House. A basement museum at the theater displays the clothes Lincoln was wearing and the weapon Booth used, as well as his diary.

Fort Sumter National Monument

Charleston, S.C.

The First Military Engagement

For two days, on April 12 and 13, 1861, Fort Sumter (below) in Charleston Harbor was under heavy bombardment until the Confederates forced the surrender of Federal troops on April 14. Major Robert Anderson (above) was widely hailed throughout the North for his determined defense of Fort Sumter. He later helped to recruit Union troops in his home state of Kentucky.

Through the night of April 11, 1861, and into the early morning hours of April 12, Captain Abner Doubleday of the U.S. Army slept soundly in his cot in one of the brick-walled gun rooms of Fort Sumter. At the same time, Doubleday's commander at the fort, Major Robert Anderson, pursued a series of last-minute negotiations with Confederate officials, attempting to stop the threatened bombardment of this Federal military post. By 3:15 A.M., however, talks had broken off and word had come from the Confederate commanders that the firing upon Fort Sumter would begin in one hour.

Awakened from his sleep, Captain Doubleday took the news with considerable calm—or so he recalled in his postwar reminiscences. "Finding it was determined not to return the fire until after breakfast," he wrote, "I remained in bed."

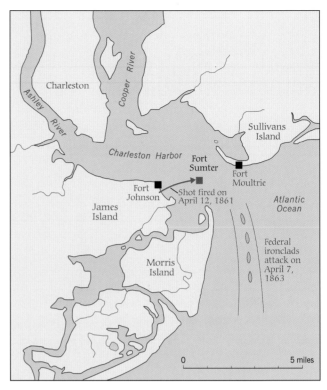

In the meantime, Confederate General Pierre Beauregard, a former student of Major Anderson at the United States Military Academy at West Point, had been preparing his troops for the assault against the Federal fortification. With troops stationed on nearby outposts and gun-carrying vessels positioned throughout Charleston Harbor, Beauregard fired upon his one-time instructor and the fortifications Anderson and his troops occupied.

Samuel Wylie Crawford, the U.S. Army surgeon stationed at the fort, recalled the approaching engagement. "Fires were lighted in all the Confederate works," Crawford remembered, "when at 4:30 [A. M.], the silence was broken by the discharge of a mortar from a battery near Fort Johnson. . . . A shell rose high in the air and burst directly over Fort Sumter." That bursting shell turned the long-standing feud between Southern slave-owners and the Federal government into a tangible and terrifying field of battle.

The election of Abraham Lincoln the previous November had prompted seven Southern states to secede —withdraw officially from the Federal Union. They feared that the election of a Republican president would mean the end of Southern influence in the national government and the eventual demise of the slave system. Leaders throughout the South had begun the process that led to secession.

On December 20, 1860, South Carolina became the first state to secede. Armed militiamen and hostile politicians in the South immediately began to direct their attention toward Major Anderson and his Federal troops, most of whom at this time occupied Fort Moultrie in Charleston Harbor. Fort Moultrie was close to the mainland and vulnerable to attack, so before the end of the year, Anderson moved his garrison of 76 soldiers, 43 workmen and 8 musicians, into the fortifications at the nearby, and more secure, Fort Sumter.

By February 1861, following the formation of a new government, known as the Confederate States of America, Anderson's crisis had intensified. With Lincoln not yet in office, the new Confederate government began to seize Federal properties that were situated inside the borders of the seceded states. They sought to establish their right to control U.S. arsenals, mints, customs houses, and forts for their own purposes. Indeed, the Confederate South Carolinians occupied Fort Moultrie, as soon as it had been vacated by Major Anderson and his troops.

Throughout January, South Carolina's governor continued to pressure the men at Fort Sumter to surrender. Major Anderson refused, despite a dwindling food supply. Soon after Lincoln's inauguration in March, the

The bombardment of Fort Sumter left the officers' quarters (left) and the soldier's barracks (right) in ruins.

Fort Sumter National Monument

1214 Middle Street
(Visitors Center)
Sullivan's Island, SC 29482
843-883-3123
www.nps.gov/fosu

NRIS 66000101
NPS

DATE BUILT
Construction began in 1829, but remained unfinished in 1860

ARCHITECT/BUILDER
U.S. Army Corps of Engineers

SIGNIFICANCE
On April 12 and 13, 1861, the first shots of the Civil War were fired at Fort Sumter as the U.S. government attempted to reprovision it. After thirty-four hours of fighting, Confederate forces captured the fort. During the last two years of the war, the fort was under a twenty-two-month siege and was reduced to brick and rubble. Also included in the Fort Sumter site is Morris Island, which was once home to Battery Wagner—the scene of a famous assault by the black troops of the Fifty-fourth Regiment of Massachusetts Volunteer Infantry.

Confederate government became anxious to remove the Federal presence from their midst and turned their attention to Fort Pickens, on the coast of Florida, and Fort Sumter.

Both sides needed this fort to show the world their legitimacy. The Confederates, anxious to stand independently before the world, greatly desired to take Fort Sumter as their own. With the United States flag still flying over this tiny piece of property, the Washington administration could still claim governing rights over the seceded states. Holed up in Charleston Harbor, perhaps the most fervently prosecessionist spot in the South, Major Anderson and his men stood as symbols of Union defiance in the face of encroaching hostilities. Symbolism aside, however, Major Anderson and his men face the threat of starvation.

Despite being a hotly contested property, Fort Sumter was hardly the most desirable military fortification at the time of the bombardment. Construction had begun in 1829 on a man-made island near the entrance to Charleston Harbor, largely in response to concerns for a stronger coastal defense system following the War of 1812.

The three-story brick fort, made from New England granite, was designed with five sides and encompassed almost two-and-a-half acres. Four of the five surrounding walls housed two tiers of enclosed gun rooms, as well as a third level with open gun platforms. The fifth wall held the entrance, the officers' quarters, eight storage rooms for ammunition and weapons, and more open gun platforms on top. There were also enlisted men's barracks next to the gun rooms on the right and left flanks of the fort.

When Anderson moved his men into Fort Sumter, the site was certainly not in a state of military readiness; it was, in fact, still under construction. "Fort Sumter," wrote one of Major Anderson's men, "was unfinished, and the interior was filled with building materials, guns, carriages, shot, shell, derricks, timbers, blocks and tackle, and coils of rope in great confusion. Few guns were mounted, and these few were chiefly on the lowest tier." When Anderson's men arrived in December of 1860, they met a surprised group of construction workers, who had scarcely expected to see troops stationed in this unfinished fortification.

The months between Anderson's occupation of Fort Sumter and the eventual eruption of hostilities in April were filled with tense maneuverings on the part of both the Federal and Confederate governments. Although his troops did proceed to outfit the fort with more weaponry, Anderson was under strict orders from Washington to make no aggressive moves against the secessionists.

Lincoln's secretary of state, William Seward, had made promises to Confederate negotiators that Fort Sumter would eventually be given up. But Lincoln himself tended toward a different view of the matter. He feared that the surrender of Fort Sumter would only weaken whatever pro-Union sentiment existed in the South, especially in those slave states that had not yet joined the secessionist movement. Believing he needed to prove to these wavering Southerners the strength of the Union, Lincoln did not wish to back down.

Thus, the new president supported a plan in which a troop transport ship, escorted by warships, would enter Charleston Harbor, but only to bring supplies to Anderson and his men. Lincoln would then inform the governor of South Carolina that the Federal government intended only to resupply hungry troops—thereby leaving it up to the Confederacy to strike an aggressive blow.

The Confederate government accepted Lincoln's challenge. On April 9, 1861, they decided to force the evacuation of Fort Sumter before the Federal supply fleet arrived. After Major Anderson refused General

After the surrender of Union forces at Fort Sumter, the fort was controlled by the Confederate troops, who raised their own flag over this military outpost.

Beauregard's demand to surrender, the Confederate general opened fire.

In fact, the Union supply ships had arrived just outside of Charleston as the firing began on the morning of April 12. However, under orders from Secretary Seward, the most powerful warship that had accompanied the fleet had been diverted from Fort Sumter and sent to Fort Pickens. Consequently, the ships that reached Charleston Harbor came unprepared and unable to assist Anderson and his men during the attack. Realizing the limited ammunition he possessed, Major Anderson and his men withstood the bombardment and offered no retaliation for close to three hours. Finally, Captain Doubleday fired back at about 7:30 A.M., but to no avail.

For the next thirty-three hours, the Confederate barrage continued as four thousand shells ripped into Fort Sumter's exterior, causing damage to the brick walls and setting off numerous fires throughout the structure. No fatalities occurred, though, until the final surrender on April 14. Then, during a one-hundred-gun salute that accompanied the lowering of the U.S. flag, an accidental explosion caused the deaths of two U.S. soldiers, the first of the more than six hundred thousand deaths that would occur over the four years of the Civil War.

Fort Sumter's significance goes beyond its position as the first point of military conflict between the North and the South. The shots exchanged there provided a catalyst for the rest of the nation, not just the military personnel, to prepare themselves for war.

Mary Ashton Livermore, a forty-one-year-old mother and reformer, was in Boston in April 1861, caring for her ailing father. News of the assault, she recalled in her postwar memoir, "fell on the land like a thunderbolt." She recorded "vigorous speech," urging war against Southerners, resounded through Boston's streets and even from the city's clergy. "There was an end of patience, and in its stead was aroused a determination to avenge the insult offered the nation."

President Lincoln tapped into precisely these emotions, which reverberated in cities and small towns throughout the North. Two days after the Fort Sumter attack, he issued a call for "the militia of the several states of the Union, to the aggregate number of seventy-five thousand to . . . maintain the honor, integrity, and existence of our National Union."

The Confederate firing on the fort was now interpreted in the North as a declaration of war, an aggressive assault by Southern enemies, which demanded a response from those who stood by the Union. Across the Northern states, men poured forth into volunteer units in response to Lincoln's call.

Throughout the South, white men and women celebrated the news of Fort Sumter's surrender. Cheered by the news of Confederate defiance and success, secessionists in four slave states—Virginia, North Carolina, Tennessee, and Arkansas—rallied behind the Confederacy and used the exuberance of the moment to lead their states out of the Union. In Charleston, the attack was greeted with enthusiasm and jubilation by local whites. Scores of Charleston ladies stepped out of their homes on the morning of the attack to watch and cheer from the city's wharves.

As the Confederate victory over the Union troops became apparent, the women were fired with glee for the Southern cause. "How gay we were last night!" wrote Charlestonian Mary Chesnut, a famous Southern diarist,

The Confederate attack on Fort Sumter aroused a tremendous response from Unionists, who rallied from across the Northern states to come to the defense of the Union. Although the Capitol dome (at the center) in Washington, D.C, was still under construction, the artist no doubt believed a completed dome would present a more inspiring image.

following the first day's bombardment. The triumph at Fort Sumter ignited a burst of patriotism that would burn fiercely in the hearts of many Southern women, at least for the first several months of the war.

To an extent, the secession crisis and the attack on Fort Sumter had obscured some of the essential factors that had brought the nation to war. As the slave states voted to leave the Union and as the Confederacy sought to establish its control over Federal property, Southerners rallied behind their right to defend their state and regional independence. In turn, Lincoln had to lead the Northerners into a defense of the Union and national sovereignty. The issue that had forced the crisis to a head—the presence and the expansion of slavery—seemed, at least momentarily, to have receded.

Or had it? African Americans, in the North and the South, recognized the profound implications that Fort Sumter had for the future of Southern slavery. The nation's foremost black leader, the ex-slave Frederick Douglass, having grown weary and impatient during the winter of secession, now saw Fort Sumter as the beginning of a "tremendous revolution in all things pertaining to the possible future" of black Americans. "God be praised," Douglass exclaimed in response to the attack. "If the Government is not yet on the side of the oppressed, events mightier than the Government are bringing about that result."

Southern slaves were more reserved in their expressions of hopefulness. But they, too, saw possibilities in the crisis in Charleston Harbor. Aware of this, Mary Chesnut

The original print of this view of Fort Sumter bore the inscription of General Pierre Beauregard, the Confederate commander, who captured the fort in April, 1861.

took time away from her celebration of the Confederate victory to cast a worried eye toward her own bondsmen:

> Not by one word or look can we detect any change in the demeanor of these Negro servants. Lawrence sits at our door, sleepy and respectful, and profoundly indifferent. So are they all, but they carry it too far. . . . Are they stolidly stupid? Or wiser than we are; silent and strong, biding their time?

Most slaves, not just Chesnut's, were certainly biding their time. Robert Smalls, for one, waited until the following spring. In May 1862, Smalls, a South Carolina slave, took hold of a dispatch boat inside Charleston Harbor, sailed it past Fort Sumter, and delivered it to the U.S. fleet outside Charleston. He had penetrated what had previously been an impenetrable ring of defensive fortifications that surrounded Charleston. Fort Sumter remained in Confederate hands, but Unionists celebrated Smalls and his skill at piercing the tight wall of security in this fiercely secessionist seaport.

For much of the war, Fort Sumter remained the object of fierce bombardment by Union forces. By the end of 1863, the fort had become little more than a pile of rubble on an earthen fortification, damaged not only by shell and mortar but by intense fires as well. Yet not until February 1865, did Fort Sumter return to the hands of the U.S. government. On April 14, 1865—five days after Confederate General Robert E. Lee surrendered to General Ulysses S. Grant, and four years to the day following the initial surrender of the fort—Major General Robert Anderson (he was promoted during the war), accompanied by numerous dignitaries and federal government officials, returned to Fort Sumter to raise the same flag he had been forced to remove. Previously a symbol of the Union's rupture, Fort Sumter became a symbol of the country's early steps toward reunification.

The fort was partially reconstructed during the 1870s. Then, during the Spanish-American War in 1898 and 1899, it was outfitted with a new artillery site, on which more accurate cannons were mounted. In 1948, both Fort Sumter and the new artillery site were acquired by the National Park Service, which over the years has done various excavations and reconstructions to create an interesting and accessible site for visitors.

RELATED SITES

FORT MOULTRIE NATIONAL MONUMENT
1214 Middle Street
(Visitors Center)
Sullivan's Island, SC 29482
843-883-3123
www.nps.gov/fomo
NPS

The first decisive victory in the American Revolution occurred at Fort Moultrie. During the Civil War, it was occupied, then vacated, by Union troops just before the attack on Fort Sumter in April 1861. The fort that now stands was built in 1809. It is the third fort on this site.

FORT PICKENS
1801 Gulf Breeze Parkway
Gulf Breeze, FL 32561
850-934-2600
www.nps.gov/guis/FortPick.htm
NPS

Fort Pickens is part of Gulf Islands National Seashore. It was built between 1829 and 1834 by the U.S. Army, with slave labor, to fortify Pensacola Harbor. After repelling a group of men, who tried to take it over in January 1861, the Union held this fort throughout the Civil War. It has been altered significantly since the Civil War era and was in use until the 1940s.

The White House of the Confederacy (Museum of the Confederacy)

Richmond, Va.

The South's Social and Political Center

Jefferson Davis (above) served as the first and only President of the Confederate States of America. Two years into the war, Davis faced increasing opposition within the South, including from his own vice-president, who called him "my poor old blind and deaf dog." The Confederate White House (below) stood on a tranquil and relatively unsettled terrain in Richmond, Virginia.

In 1861, Richmond, Virginia, stood as the chief city of the state, despite being a provincial center with about forty thousand inhabitants. Divided by a tributary of the James River, the city occupied the hills and gullies on either side of this waterway, covering a territory of approximately three-and-a-half square miles. With most of Richmond's sizable free black population residing on the outskirts of the city, the central hills of Richmond were home to the city's elites and public officials. After May 1861, the leaders of the Confederate government also made Richmond their home.

Virginia's recent decision to join the newly formed Confederate States of America had prompted Confederate officials to move the government from its deep South

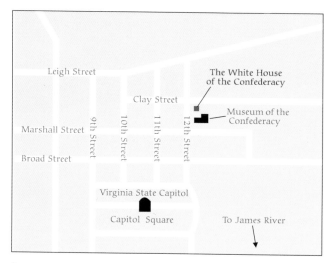

location in Montgomery, Alabama, to the upper South location of Richmond. Such a move, they hoped, would strengthen the place of Virginia, the South's most populous and industrialized state in the Confederacy. Thus, one month after the firing on Fort Sumter in April 1861, the Confederate Congress and other Southern officials began conducting their business in this Virginia city. Likewise, Confederate President Jefferson Davis, along with his family, prepared to take up residency in this new capitol.

To prepare for the arrival of the Davis family, the city leaders acquired what they believed was a suitable home for the Confederate head of state. The Brockenbrough mansion, as it was known, had been built in 1818 by the architect Robert Mills, who later designed the Washington Monument, the Treasury Building, and the U.S. Patent Office. It was originally constructed as a two-story dwelling for Dr. John Brockenbrough, a prominent physician and bank president.

The home had been enlarged in 1844 by its fourth owner, Lewis Crenshaw, a wealthy Richmond merchant. Crenshaw added a third story, as well as gas-burning chandeliers and various ornamental fixtures. He transformed a fairly simple Greek Revival home into an elegant mansion. The gray-stuccoed brick house with a columned porch stood at the corner of Clay and Twelfth streets. It was on one of the hills occupied by well-to-do Richmond families, overlooking what one local resident described as "a landscape of romantic beauty."

To convey their welcome to the Confederate chief, the city of Richmond bought the house from Crenshaw

Architect Robert Mills designed the Brockenbrough mansion, later known as the Confederate White House, as well as several Washington, D.C. landmarks. He was commemorated in this 1936 plaster plaque that was commissioned by the U.S. Treasury.

The White House of the Confederacy (Museum of the Confederacy)

1201 East Clay Street
Richmond, VA 23219
804-649-1861
www.moc.org

NRIS 66000924
NHL

DATE BUILT
1818

ARCHITECT
Robert Mills

SIGNIFICANCE
This gray-stuccoed brick building was the official residence of Confederate President Jefferson Davis and his family from 1861 to 1865. It was mainly a site for family and social activities for the Confederacy's first family, until it was seized by Union forces at the very end of the war. Today it is a museum of the history of the Confederacy.

for $35,000 and then offered it as a gift. Davis, however, declined the offer. Instead, the Confederate government rented the home for the Davis family, complete with elegant furnishings provided by wealthy Richmond ladies, for the duration of the Civil War.

By the summer of 1861, Jefferson Davis, his wife Varina, and their children had established themselves in this site known today, though inaccurately, as the White House of the Confederacy. Never an explicitly political site, the Davis mansion functioned more as a social center for both the Davis family and Confederate society. Although Jefferson Davis spent considerable time in his home, agonizing over the political and military fate of the Confederacy, his wife Varina dominated the domestic life of this executive mansion and the social life of wartime Richmond.

Born in 1826, Varina Howell Davis, in many ways, epitomized the problems and opportunities that were part of the lives of elite Southern women. She spent her girlhood on a large Mississippi plantation, where she learned to love fine clothes and graceful living. As the oldest daughter, she also assumed considerable responsibility for the welfare of her siblings. She received a more extensive education than most Southern girls, that included schooling at a young ladies' academy in Philadelphia. However, in elite and conservative Southern circles, her learning marked her as rather unfeminine. She faced a future with few choices beside marriage.

At the age of nineteen, she married Jefferson Davis, a man seventeen years her senior. In 1861, she became the mistress of the White House of the Confederacy and First Lady of the Confederacy. She was thirty-five, a mother of four children and pregnant with her fifth. Considered by some to be rather matronly and imperial, she was occasionally referred to as "Queen Varina."

Despite her pregnancy, Varina worked quickly to establish the White House of the Confederacy as a suitable place to receive visitors and hold social functions. Hungry for witty and fashionable company, Mrs. Davis made the Confederate mansion, at least in the first year of the war, a gathering place for intelligent and entertaining Southern aristocrats. She remained "at home" every Tuesday evening to receive visitors and held receptions every two weeks.

At these gatherings she enjoyed the companionship of various Confederate dignitaries and officers, including Confederate Secretary of State Judah Benjamin, and Mary Chesnut, who beside being a Southern diarist was also the wife of one of President Davis's aides. To these social events, remarked the former Washington journalist Thomas DeLeon:

> flocked 'the world and his wife,' in what holiday attire they possessed, in the earlier days marked by the dainty toilettes of really elegant women, the butternut [-colored uniform] of the private soldier, and the stars and yellow sashes of many a general, already world-famous.

Some objected to these gatherings, which seemed to imitate the parties in the Lincoln White House. Others believed Varina overdid her role as society hostess, behaving in a manner that was inappropriate to the role of a demure Southern wife. The parlors of the Confederate mansion, complained Varina's sister-in-law, were "filled with strange gentlemen" and "[a] few ladies," all of whom were greeted and received by the self-assured Varina.

Varina Davis was thirty-five-years-old and pregnant when she came to preside, as First Lady, over the so-called Confederate White House in Richmond, Virginia. She quickly made her home a gathering place for leading Southern ladies and men.

Soon after moving into his new home, Jefferson Davis converted a bedroom into a home office, where he could work and receive visitors for all types of business. In June 1862, he held a meeting in this room with General Robert E. Lee and General Thomas "Stonewall" Jackson.

The Davis family owned considerable property, in both land and slaves, prior to the Civil War. The slaves shown here were probably owned by Jefferson Davis's niece, on her plantation, south of Vicksburg, Mississippi.

The Confederate White House also witnessed Varina's various trials and tribulations as a Southern wife and mother. The housekeeping alone required considerable effort, especially in wartime Richmond. A family member believed that Varina, in particular, felt the strain of keeping up appearances, especially since it was so difficult to "get suitable servants, everything double the price." Perhaps more serious than the price of good help was the fact that slavery in Richmond—as in the rest of the Confederacy—was a doomed institution, gradually disintegrating as the war progressed.

Throughout the city, the most trusted maids and house servants had begun to flee their masters' homes, many of them seeking refuge with Federal troops. The Davises, who had brought some slaves with them from Mississippi and then purchased others in Richmond, found themselves similarly deserted by their bondsmen and women. One winter day in 1864, when a fire broke out in the basement of the Confederate White House and a supply of groceries was stolen in the process, suspicions turned immediately to Davis's family servants.

By January 1864, President Davis's personal servant Jim, as well as Varina's maid Betsy, had run away. Mary Chesnut believed this was an inevitable event, given the opportunities provided by the Union forces. "At Mrs. Davis's," Chesnut wrote in her diary, "the hired servants are mere birds of passage. First they are seen with gold galore, and then their wings sprout, and they fly to the Yankees."

Varina bore two children in this home: her son William, born in December 1861, and daughter Varina Anne, known as "Winnie," in 1864. She also endured the tragic loss of her five-year-old son Joseph, who died in 1864 after falling from a second-story porch. In 1862, Varina and her children were forced to flee temporarily from their White House, when a Union invasion seemed imminent. The Union forces were driven back from Richmond but, like so many Southern families, Varina and her children, at least for a short time, suffered through the uncertain experience of being wartime refugees.

As the war dragged on, even Varina Davis had to adapt to a less extravagant way of living. The Union-imposed blockade made it difficult for Southerners to obtain food and supplies. Many Confederate families had to give up various goods, and even basic foodstuffs, they had once enjoyed. The items that could be obtained were often unaffordable, owing to the mounting inflation rate in the South. Ham, which previously had cost

continued on page 42

Confederate war propaganda celebrated the contributions that Southern women made to the war effort. This 1863 illustration depicts Confederate ladies making clothes for the boys in the army.

The Confederate Constitution

 The Congress of the Confederate States of South Carolina, Georgia, Florida, Alabama, Mississippi, Louisiana, and Texas, meeting in Montgomery, Alabama, on March 11, 1861, unanimously adopted a constitution that very much resembled the United States Constitution. However, it included stricter protections for the institution of slavery.

PREAMBLE

We, the people of the Confederate States, each State acting in its sovereign and independent character, in order to form a permanent federal government, establish justice, insure domestic tranquillity, and secure the blessings of liberty to ourselves and our posterity—invoking the favor and guidance of Almighty God—do ordain and establish this Constitution for the Confederate States of America.

ARTICLE I

Section 1. All legislative powers herein delegated shall be vested in a Congress of the Confederate States, which shall consist of a Senate and House of Representatives.

Section 2. (1) The House of Representatives shall be composed of members chosen every second year by the people of the several States; and the electors in each State shall be citizens of the Confederate States, and have the qualifications requisite for electors of the most numerous branch of the State Legislature; but no person of foreign birth, not a citizen of the Confederate States, shall be allowed to vote for any officer, civil or political, State or Federal.

(2) No person shall be a Representative who shall not have attained the age of twenty-five years, and be a citizen of the Confederate States, and who shall not when elected, be an inhabitant of that State in which he shall be chosen.

(3) Representatives and direct taxes shall be apportioned among the several States, which may be included within this Confederacy, according to their respective numbers, which shall be determined by adding to the whole number of free persons, including those bound to service for a term of years, and excluding Indians not taxed, three-fifths of all slaves. The actual enumeration shall be made within three years after the first meeting of the Congress of the Confederate States, and within every subsequent term of ten years, in such manner as they shall by law direct. The number of Representatives shall not exceed one for every fifty thousand, but each State shall have at least one Representative; and until such enumeration shall be made, the State of South Carolina shall be entitled to choose six; the State of Georgia ten; the State of Alabama nine; the State of Florida two; the State of Mississippi seven; the State of Louisiana six; and the State of Texas six.

Section 9. (1) The importation of negroes of the African race from any foreign country other than the slaveholding States or Territories of the United States of America, is hereby forbidden; and Congress is required to pass such laws as shall effectually prevent the same.

(2) Congress shall also have power to prohibit the introduction of slaves from any State not a member of, or Territory not belonging to, this Confederacy.

(3) The privilege of the writ of habeas corpus shall not be suspended, unless when in cases of rebellion or invasion the public safety may require it.

(4) No bill of attainder, ex post facto law, or

law denying or impairing the right of property in negro slaves shall be passed. . . .

ARTICLE II

Section 1. (1) The executive power shall be vested in a President of the Confederate States of America. He and the Vice President shall hold their offices for the term of six years; but the President shall not be reeligible. The President and Vice President shall be elected as follows. . . .

ARTICLE III

Section 1. (1) The judicial power of the Confederate States shall be vested in one Supreme Court, and in such inferior courts as the Congress may, from time to time, ordain and establish. The judges, both of the Supreme and inferior courts, shall hold their offices during good behavior, and shall, at stated times, receive for their services a compensation which shall not be diminished during their continuance in office. . . .

ARTICLE IV

Section 1. (1) Full faith and credit shall be given in each State to the public acts, records, and judicial proceedings of every other State; and the Congress may, by general laws, prescribe the manner in which such acts, records, and proceedings shall be proved, and the effect thereof.

Section 2. (1) The citizens of each State shall be entitled to all the privileges and immunities of citizens in the several States; and shall have the right of transit and sojourn in any State of this Confederacy, with their slaves and other property; and the right of property in said slaves shall not be thereby impaired.

(2) A person charged in any State with treason, felony, or other crime against the laws of such State, who shall flee from justice, and be found in another State, shall, on demand of the executive authority of the State from which he fled, be delivered up, to be removed to the State having jurisdiction of the crime.

(3) No slave or other person held to service or labor in any State or Territory of the Confederate States, under the laws thereof, escaping or lawfully carried into another, shall, in consequence of any law or regulation therein, be discharged from such service or labor; but shall be delivered up on claim of the party to whom such slave belongs, or to whom such service or labor may be due. . . .

ARTICLE VII

The ratification of the conventions of five States shall be sufficient for the establishment of this Constitution between the States so ratifying the same.

When five States shall have ratified this Constitution, in the manner before specified, the Congress under the Provisional Constitution shall prescribe the time for holding the election of President and Vice President; and for the meeting of the Electoral College; and for counting the votes, and inaugurating the President. They shall, also, prescribe the time for holding the first election of members of Congress under this Constitution, and the time for assembling the same. Until the assembling of such Congress, the Congress under the Provisional Constitution shall continue to exercise the legislative powers granted them; not extending beyond the time limited by the Constitution of the Provisional Government.

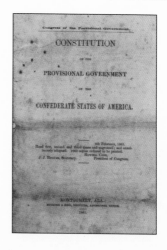

continued from page 39

75¢, sold for as much as $7 a pound. The cost of chickens had risen from 57¢ to $12 for a pair. "The family of the President," Varina explained, "had no prerequisites and bought their provender [food] as they did their [other] provisions, at the public marts and at the current prices."

Nonetheless, the First Lady tried to maintain a social atmosphere and even introduced a new form of entertainment in the Confederate White House, amid the hard times of 1863. These "matinee musicales," as they were called, made use of Richmond's amateur musicians and singers, with the guests often joining in for songs and poetry readings. But the days of these simplified forms of entertainment were rapidly drawing to a close.

In the spring of 1865, with the war nearing its conclusion and a Confederate defeat appearing all but certain, Varina and her family evacuated the Confederate presidential mansion for good. The Union troops persued them and caught up with the family in southwestern Georgia. There, they arrested and imprisoned Jefferson Davis.

As the Davises and others evacuated Richmond, Confederates set fire to significant portions of their capital,

As news came of the imminent Union occupation of their city, thousands fled Richmond on April 2, 1865, leaving the city in the hands of mobs, who looted and burned the Confederate capital. When Union soldiers entered Richmond the next day, they put out the fires.

The Alabama State Capitol (First Confederate Capitol)

Between February and May 1861, the state capitol building in Montgomery, Alabama, served as the focal point for Confederate politics. A deep South state with a strong dependence on slavery, Alabama had been one of the first states to secede from the Union.

On January 11, 1861, soon after secession had been approved in South Carolina, Mississippi, and Florida, an Alabama Secession Convention met in this capitol building and cast the state's fate with the secession movement. Three states—Georgia, Louisiana, and Texas—followed soon after. On February 4, delegates from the seven seceded states convened at the Montgomery site and by February 8, arrived at a unanimous agreement on a constitution for the newly created Confederate States of America. For the next three months, Confederate decision making emanated from the Montgomery headquarters.

February 18, 1862, marked a significant occasion for the new Confederate capital, in particular the Montgomery building. Here, Jefferson Davis was inaugurated as President of the Confederate States of America. A former U.S. Senator from Mississippi, and a more moderate secessionist than some of his compatriots, Davis had received the unanimous support of Southern delegates in his bid for the Confederate presidency.

His inauguration buoyed the hopes and enthusiasm of white Southerners in what seemed to be the dawning of Southern independence. "All Montgomery had flocked to Capitol Hill in holiday attire," wrote one Southern journalist on the day of the inaugural celebration. Davis addressed a cheering and excited crowd, and the first Confederate flag, the Stars and Bars, made its initial public appearance as it was flown above the Confederate Capitol building.

The building that provided the focal point for these activities was the second structure to occupy the site on top of Goat Hill, at the head of Montgomery's main business street. The original building was destroyed in a fire in 1849. The second building was completed in October 1851. Based on a simple design, this square-shaped structure included an exterior dome and covered porch; inside, it provided meeting rooms for the Alabama Senate and House of Representatives. Its main architectural highlights are the double spiral staircases that rise two stories inside the main entrance, and the finely designed rotunda.

Confederate congressmen continued to convene in their Alabama headquarters until May 22, 1861. Following the bombardment of Fort Sumter, the Confederacy welcomed delegates from four more Southern states: Virginia, Tennessee, North Carolina, and Arkansas. Anxious to secure their ties to these upper South states, especially to the more populous and industrialized state of Virginia, the Southern Congress accepted the invitation of Virginia's secession convention to move the capital of the Confederate government to Richmond.

New wings were added to the Montgomery building in the late-nineteenth and early-twentieth centuries. A complete renovation was done in the 1930s. During this time, the building and its grounds, often referred to as the "Cradle of the Confederacy," offered some Southern whites a location for memorializing the leaders and soldiers of the Confederate government. Near the west portico of the capitol stands a bronze statue of Jefferson Davis. A large marble monument, erected in the 1890s as a tribute to Confederate sailors and soldiers, occupies a portion of the north lawn. The building still functions today as the seat of Alabama state politics.

determined to slow the progress of the advancing Union army. The fire was primarily confined to the business and warehouse districts of the city and thus the White House of the Confederacy was spared from the flames.

On April 2, 1865, Federal officers established temporary headquarters in the former Davis family home. Two days later, President Lincoln journeyed to Richmond and paid a visit to the mansion that just forty hours previously had been occupied by his Confederate counterpart. As the story goes, he even took a seat in the study, musing that he now sat in what "must have been President Davis's chair." The house that once stood as a symbol of the Confederate quest for independence came to symbolize the finality of the Federal victory over the South.

The Brockenbrough mansion remained in the hands of the U.S. government between 1865 and 1870 and was returned to the city of Richmond in 1870. It served as a school between 1878 and 1893. By the 1890s, the site had captured the attention of Southern whites, who were interested in honoring and celebrating the Confederate past. The building was acquired in 1893 by the Confederate Memorial Literary Society, an organization devoted to remembering the South's "lost cause." Under society ownership, the site became the repository for numerous Confederate artifacts, including the swords of Robert E. Lee and Stonewall Jackson. Today, the house is a part of the Museum of the Confederacy.

After the Union took control of Richmond, Virginia, Abraham Lincoln visited the Confederate White House on April 3, 1865. Greeting crowds of freed slaves wherever he went, Lincoln heard one woman shout, "I know I am free for I have seen Father Abraham and felt him."

ALABAMA STATE CAPITOL

Dexter Avenue
Montgomery, AL 36104
800-151-2262
www.state.al.us
NHL

Built in 1851 by Barachias Holt, the building was the first Confederate Capitol. On February 8, 1861, the Constitution of the Confederate States of America was adopted in this building by thirty-seven delegates from seven southern states. The Confederacy's new president, Jefferson Davis, was inaugurated on the west portico on February 18, with the Confederate flag flying for the first time over this building (as shown in the frontispiece of this book). The Confederate Congress met here until May 22, 1861, when the capital was moved to Richmond, Virginia.

Jefferson Davis and his family occupied this home—known as Beauvoir—from 1877 to 1889.

BEAUVOIR

2244 Beach Boulevard
Biloxi, MS 39531
228-388-9074,
800-570-3818
www.beauvoir.org
NHL

This home, built between 1848 and 1851, was given to Jefferson Davis by a Mississippi widow Sarah Dorsey in 1877. Dorsey named the estate Beauvoir, meaning "beautiful view" for the view of Mississippi Sound from the house. Davis lived here with his family until his death in 1889.

VIRGINIA STATE CAPITOL

Capitol Square
Richmond, VA 23219
804-698-1788
www.state.va.us
NHL

The Virginia State Capitol, designed by Thomas Jefferson and architect Louis Clerisseau, served as the state capitol for seventy years, until Virginia seceded from the Union in 1861. From July 1861 to April 1865, the building housed the Confederate Congress, and served as the Confederate Capitol.

Manassas National Battlefield Park

Manassas, Va.

A Battleground for Soldiers and Journalists

General Thomas J. Jackson (above) emerged as one of the Confederacy's preeminent commanders at the First Battle of Bull Run. While holding his ground on the battlefield, Jackson earned the enduring nickname, "Stonewall."

B y the end of May 1861, a mood of impatience had begun to settle on many Unionists. Nearly six weeks had passed since the Civil War had begun with the fall of Fort Sumter, and little action had been taken to squelch the Southern rebellion. In the meantime, the Confederacy had defiantly moved its capitol to Richmond, Virginia, a city only one hundred miles from Washington, D.C. The likelihood of a clash between Northern and Southern troops, somewhere between Washington and Richmond, seemed imminent. But as the month of June arrived and little movement could be detected, uneasiness in the North increased.

Among the most restless were the region's newspaper reporters. Fitz Henry Warren, the Washington correspondent for the *New York Tribune,* loudly led the growing chorus of Northerners, who began to pressure the Lincoln administration to take action against the South. "To Richmond Onward!" wrote Warren in the *New York Tribune's* pages, "On to Richmond . . . is the voice of the people. . . . " When, in late June, the Confederate Congress declared that it would meet in Richmond on July 20, 1861, and still little action had been taken against the city, Warren, along with *New York Tribune* editor Horace Greeley, turned up the heat. On June 22, the *New York Tribune's* editorial page proclaimed: "Forward to Richmond! The Rebel Congress must not be allowed to meet there on the 20th of July!"

As it turned out, the Union Army began its move into Virginia by late July and ensued the battle, referred to by Northerners as the First Battle of Bull Run, named for the stream that ran through the area. Southerners would identify the battle that took place there by the town's name, Manassas.

Lincoln, his military advisors, and his commanding officers played a role in orchestrating the maneuvers into Virginia. However, the *New York Tribune* and several other papers gave voice to a growing popular desire to avenge the nation's honor for the Confederate attack on Fort Sumter. In this way, they encouraged the Lincoln administration to reject the less aggressive solutions to the secession crisis, and advanced the North more quickly into an open military engagement.

Although they decided not to move immediately "on to Richmond," Lincoln and his aides made plans to proceed against the twenty thousand Confederate troops positioned along a six-mile stretch of Bull Run. These troops were guarding an important railroad junction at Manassas, not far from Richmond. Led by Pierre Beauregard, the Confederates at Manassas protected both the Orange and Alexandria railroad line, which led to Richmond, and the Manassas Gap railroad, which led west into the Shenandoah Valley, and the Confederate troops stationed there under Joseph Johnston.

Union General Irvin McDowell, the commander of the thirty-five thousand troops massed in Washington, conceived of a plan to lead his men down the Orange and Alexandria line and then launch an attack on the Confederates at Manassas Junction. The success of this maneuver would require preventing Johnston's troops in the west from providing support for the Confederates in Manassas. If successful, McDowell would not only hand

This section of the Manassas battlefield photographed in a moment of tranquility in 1862, had swarmed with Union soldiers during the Battle of Bull Run the previous July. The soldiers' hopes of filling their canteens here became frustrated when they discovered that the water had become too muddy from the constant tramping of thousands of soldiers.

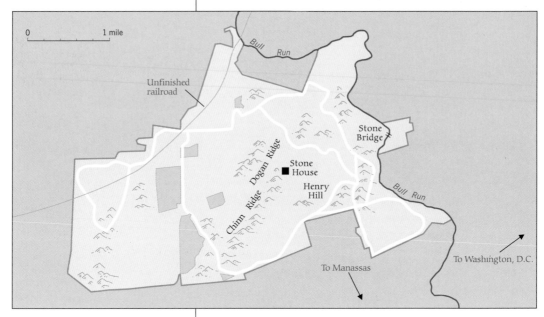

a defeat to the main body of the Confederate troops in the east, he would also be within striking distance of the Confederate capital.

Although they knew little about the Virginia terrain and the Manassas region, the Northern press became immersed in the unfolding developments, ferreting out whatever information they could on the location and activities of the Union troops. Sometimes the press revealed too much about army movements and military strategy.

The reporters were a motley crew. Participating in a new and often ridiculed profession, the journalists in 1861 operated in a field with almost no rules or standards. Few made any attempts to disguise their personal biases and opinions. Many loudly advertised their loyalty to a particular political party.

In the North, Civil War newsmen began to proclaim themselves part of a "Bohemian" brigade, a reference to their decidedly marginal and sometimes suspect position in their society. Whether attached to small-town journals or big-city dailies, all were intent on selling their papers with whatever war information could be procured, even if it was highly sensitive or grossly inaccurate. Still throughout the country they had access to one of the most significant technological breakthroughs of the era: the telegraph. With the ability to send their dispatches to their editors immediately, these reporters would make Civil War one of the first instant-news wars in history.

In the early months of the war, telegraph wires began to buzz with information, much of it coming from Northern reporters, who were often overzealous in sending as much news as possible back to their papers. To restrain some of this early enthusiasm, the Federal government imposed a policy of censorship on reporters. The censors, no doubt did too much, occasionally discarding entire news dispatches that had only a single unacceptable point.

The censorship policy ceased toward the end of June 1861, just as news was beginning to circulate of the Manassas campaign. By July, General McDowell had even agreed to allow reporters to accompany his army and joked to a *London Times* correspondent that the newsmen "should wear a white uniform to indicate the purity of their character."

In contrast to the fairly strict supervision exercised by the Union government over the Northern press, the Confederacy took a relatively lenient view of Southern newspapers. Throughout the war, journals in the South enjoyed an almost complete freedom of editorial expression, a right they exercised extensively in numerous criticisms registered against the Confederate government. Some military information was suppressed. But this was done more by individual army commanders than as the result of any consistent government policy. Still, by mid-July of 1861, Southern reporters were finding it increasingly difficult to obtain and forward reliable information about the military situation in Virginia.

By now the Confederate government controlled all the telegraph lines north of Richmond and could stem the flow of news about army maneuvers. Reporters often heard only rumors, mistaken for actual news, about troop movements in Virginia. And as few reporters actually knew where the army was, few eyewitnesses were around to view the military activity. As a result, small skirmishes would often be described as full-scale battles. By July 20, however, a few journalists did manage to get to Manassas, including two of the South's leading war correspondents, Peter Alexander of the *Savannah Republican* and Felix Gregory de Fontaine of the *Charleston Courier.*

As they approached Manassas Junction, the reporters must have thought it an unlikely spot for military conflict. Only the presence of the railroad line would

The Union army relied heavily on telegraph operators so that troops in the field could stay in constant communication with army headquarters. The telegraph became critical for wartime correspondents too, enabling them to send news from the battlefields to their home offices.

Manassas National Battlefield Park

12521 Lee Highway
Manassas, VA 20109
703-754-1861 (Headquarters)
703-361-1339 (Visitors Center)
www.nps.gov/mana

NRIS 66000039
NPS

DATE OF BATTLE
Battle of First Bull Run (First Manassas) July 21, 1861; Battle of Second Bull Run (Second Manassas) August 28-30, 1862

SIGNIFICANCE
The 1861 battle was the first major encounter of the Civil War after the shelling of Fort Sumter in April of that year. It forced people to realize that the contest would be a long one. It was also the place where Confederate Brigadier General Thomas J. Jackson acquired his nickname "Stonewall." The 1,600-acre site became a National Battlefield Park in 1940.

have suggested the site's strategic significance. Otherwise, the landscape revealed a gently rolling terrain, broken up by the Bull Run stream, the Alexandria–Warrenton turnpike, and the Manassas–Sudley Road. The well-known English correspondent William Howard Russell, following a late arrival to the battle site, described the scene as one "enclosed in a framework of blue and purple hills, softened into violet in the extreme distance." A few small, unpaved lanes also crossed the area. A red sandstone bridge, built in 1825, carried the Alexandria turnpike over Bull Run.

Most of the land they came upon was farmland, much of it used for grazing, with few trees obscuring the field of vision. A few houses dotted the landscape, including the ruins of an old mansion built by a prominent eighteenth-century Virginian Landon Carter, Jr. On a hill stood two homes of local farmers: Judith Carter Henry, a widow, lived in one and James Robinson, a free black man, occupied the second.

This would also have been the scene observed by the large group of Northern civilians, who had also traveled to the Manassas region. This Yankee contingent consisted of a significant number of curious citizens and U.S. congressmen, along with a fairly sizable group of Northern newsmen. Scarcely recognizing the dangers and the chaos of warfare, these civilians made the short drive from Washington to Manassas to get a first-hand look at the men assault each other with deadly determination.

Included in the Union journalists' band were the editors of the *New York Times* and the *Chicago Tribune;* various reporters and illustrators from Boston, New York, Rochester, Philadelphia, and Cincinnati. Also present was Mathew Brady, a pioneer in the new craft of photography and whose assistant photographers would eventually send back harrowing pictures of the dead and the wounded as the Civil War progressed.

For the most part, the Northern reporters stayed together as a group, trying to abide by Union General McDowell's directive to stay out of the way of the action. The reporters chose to stay close to the main road, which led to the telegraph station at Fairfax, thirteen miles from the battle site.

In the early morning hours of Sunday, July 21, 1861, McDowell launched the opening attack of the battle, and several reporters were there to bear witness.

Thomas Morris Chester: Reporting from the Front Line of Emancipation

Thomas Morris Chester was not among the journalists covering the battle of Manassas, and did not begin reporting on the war until much later in the conflict. Chester's reports, unlike those of the Manassas press corps, directed the public's attention to a later, and increasingly dramatic, aspect of the war: the actions of African-American troops. He also served as the nation's only black war correspondent during the Civil War.

Born in 1834 in Harrisburg, Pennsylvania, Thomas Morris Chester was the fourth child born to George and Jane Chester. His father owned a restaurant and his mother was a former slave who had escaped to Pennsylvania in the 1820s. After being raised in an abolitionist environment, Chester moved to Liberia in the 1850s as part of the colonization efforts that aimed to settle American blacks, both slave and free, in Africa. While in Liberia, he published his own newspaper and also served as the *New York Herald* correspondent from that African nation.

Chester returned to the United States when the Civil War began in 1861. An enthusiastic supporter of black enlistment in the Union army, Chester lent his voice to Frederick Douglass's efforts to recruit African-American soldiers for the Fifty-fourth and and Fifty-fifth Massachusetts Volunteer Infantry regiments. In 1864, The *Philadelphia Press* hired Chester as a war correspondent and asked him to cover the movements and activities of the Army at the James River, which flows southeast from Richmond, Virginia, to Chesapeake Bay. Writing under the pen name "Rollins," Chester paid particular attention to the conduct and concerns of black soldiers and former slaves.

When the Union army captured Richmond on April 4, 1865, Thomas Chester was one of the first correspondents to enter the city. Taking a seat in Jefferson Davis's speaker's chair in the Confederate Congress, Chester issued one of the most dramatic news reports in all of Civil War journalism. "Seated in the Speaker's chair," wrote this son of a former slave, "so long dedicated to treason, but in future to be consecrated to loyalty, I hasten to give a rapid sketch of the incidents which have occurred since my last dispatch."

Chester declined to tell the story of the Confederate officer who called him a "black cuss" and ordered him out of the hall, a demand which Chester calmly refused. But he wrote movingly of the elderly black men and women who lined Richmond's streets and welcomed the Union army of liberation into their midst.

Immediately after the war, Chester traveled throughout Europe, raising funds on behalf of a Pennsylvania freedmen's aid society. In 1867, motivated by a desire to work for the uplift of his race, Chester pursued a legal education in England and, in 1870, became the first black American admitted to the English bar. Soon after, he returned to the U. S., determined to put his skills to work on behalf of former slaves. He settled in Louisiana, where he became immersed in the heated political conflicts of the period and tried—often in vain—to uphold the civil and political rights of the state's black residents. The end of the Reconstruction era, which had been a time of some gains for former slaves, albeit limited, left Chester frustrated and disappointed. He returned to his home state and died in Pennsylvania in 1892.

Among the prominent participants in the Bull Run battle were several Union Zouave regiments, so called for the uniforms they wore based on the French Zouave troops that fought in the Crimean war.

They climbed up the trees to watch as Federal troops fired their guns and marched across the red sandstone bridge, to be known henceforth as the Stone Bridge. They watched as the troops proceeded up the hill, where the Henry and Robinson houses were situated.

They saw a constant stream of railroad cars coming along the Manassas Gap Railroad, bringing Confederate reinforcements from Johnston's army in the west. Nonetheless, by 3 P. M. the reporters, and even many soldiers, sensed a Union victory. Several Northern newsmen scampered off to file initial reports; most were optimistic.

However, the tide began to turn quickly in favor of the Confederates. General Thomas Jackson kept his men on the hill and held firm against the Union soldiers. A fellow Confederate, hoping to rally his own men, supposedly directed their attention toward Jackson and shouted, "Look! There is Jackson standing like a stone wall." Legend has it, this remark endowed Jackson with his enduring nickname of "Stonewall." In any event, Southern troops rallied behind Jackson and the Confederates managed to lead a successful counterattack. The Northern advance collapsed and the Union troops fled in a chaotic and panicked retreat.

Like all the civilians, who had come to watch the battle, the reporters became entangled in the wildly confused flight from Bull Run. Untrained Union soldiers became a panicked mob, running for their lives away from the battlefield. "A perfect frenzy was upon almost every man," wrote one reporter for the *New York Tribune*, "... Every impediment to flight was cast aside. Rifles, bayonets, pistols, haversacks, cartridge boxes, canteens, blankets, belts and overcoats lined the road." The English reporter William Howard Russell called the retreat "the Bull Run races." One Northern reporter, grabbing the flag of the Fifth Massachusetts Regiment, tried to rally the retreating soldiers behind him.

Southern reporters also became absorbed in the final frenzy of the battle. A New Orleans journalist claimed that the Confederate regiments "ran up the hill in the wild excitement of pursuit." He also heard them speak, in earnest, of pushing their campaign on "to Washington" and "to Baltimore." One especially unfortunate Confederate newsman, J. P. Pryor, strayed too close to the enemy line and was captured as a prisoner. In the meantime, *Savannah Republican* reporter Peter Alexander made it back to Manassas Junction from the battlefield and filed this report: "Glory to God in the highest!" he proclaimed. "A great battle has been fought and a victory won!"

At last, Northern reporters also grasped the truth of the events and reported to their newspapers that this first major military engagement of the Civil War had resulted in a clear-cut Union defeat. Overall, casualties were relatively light compared to what would occur later in the war: about 3,500 total dead and wounded out of nearly 71,000 engaged. The effect was nonetheless staggering to those who read the news. More than anything, the battle of First Bull Run (First Manassas to the Confederates) confirmed that the war between the North and the South would be a long and protracted contest.

This was not the extent of the bloodshed, which the nation and its news reporters would witness at Manassas Junction. A little over one year later, on August 28 through 30, 1862, the war returned to this site. This time, the battle of Second Bull Run, or Second Manassas, would consist of a series of military maneuvers in which the Confederates, now under the command of Robert E. Lee, sought to suppress the newly organized Union Army of Virginia, under the command of General John Pope.

As with First Bull Run, the news reports from this second contest revealed a state of chaos

Southern newspapers, not always able to get timely reports of military actions, sometimes relied on Northern accounts to get information to their readers. As a result, Southern readers learned of Union casualties before getting any information on their own dead and wounded.

CHRONICLE & SENTINEL
EXTRA.

NORTHERN ACCOUNTS
OF THE
BATTLE AT MANASSAS.

Five Thousand Killed & Wounded

CAPTURE OF THE RHODE ISLAND, SHERMAN'S, CARLILE'S GRIFFIN'S, AND WEST POINT BATTERIES.

Preserving Civil War Sites

Over the years, the Manassas battlefield, along with many other Civil War sites, has become embroiled in a new type of struggle regarding the preservation of its historic integrity. On the one hand, historians and visitors appreciate being able to see and experience these nineteenth-century battlefields and fortifications as the soldiers themselves did. Seeing the landscape as it would have appeared in the 1860s allows a twenty-first-century visitor to better understand the strategic importance of a particular site and the tactical considerations that influenced the way a battle was fought.

Although sections of the Gettysburg battlefield can give modern visitors an excellent idea of what this area was like in 1863, the surrounding community has changed considerably over the years, making it more difficult to preserve the nineteenth-century landscape.

However, many Civil War battlefields occupy extensive, and valuable, tracts of land. Those who wish to maintain even some of the landscape's original conditions must persistently confront the forces of modern growth and commercial development. They must continually consider the question of how much preservation of a battlefield is necessary to convey a sense of historical accuracy. They must also persistently resist the kinds of modern conveniences, such as fast-food restaurants and shopping areas, that many visitors, not to mention residents, want and appreciate.

A proposal by the Walt Disney Company to construct a high-tech historic theme park near the Manassas battlefield was defeated in the 1990s, but the battle against commercial growth remains and has, if anything, accelerated. Modern highways, suburban tract homes, and congested shopping centers now flank the boundaries of the park land. At Manassas, which today is a commuter suburb near Washington, D.C., the pressures for commercial development are especially pronounced, and the tension between preservation and growth is apparent to everyone who visits.

At Gettysburg, Pennsylvania, a site that is further removed from an urban center, recent attempts to preserve the landscape have been more successful. A tourist observation tower, long seen as an eyesore on the battlefield site, was removed in 2000. The National Park Service has embarked on an ambitious plan to create a landscape that more closely resembles the 1863 battlefield. They intend to cut down extensive groves of trees that have grown up in the past 150 years. This, they hope, will allow visitors to see how thousands of men moved across the relatively unobstructed fields and pastures in the battle.

Still, Gettysburg and other Civil War locations will continue to experience the basic problem that all historic sites face: how to preserve the sense of history that surrounds a time-honored structure or battlefield while that historic place remains in a world that continues to change and develop.

and confusion, although reporters had become more resourceful at finding ways to learn the news. Recently banished from Pope's army, several Northern journalists had disguised themselves as clerks and hospital assistants in order to stay with the troops. Nonetheless they, like Pope and his men, stumbled blindly into the trap that the Confederate troops had laid at the old Bull Run battlefield. Union newspapers blared forth initially optimistic reports heralding the capture of Stonewall Jackson. A few days later, the Northern public learned the truth of yet another Northern defeat.

As with many Civil War battlefields, over the years, the Bull Run site was memorialized by the participants and their descendants. Several monuments, paying tribute to both Union and Confederate soldiers, have been erected. At the very end of the war, in 1865, Union veterans constructed two monuments to honor their comrades, who had fallen in the first and second battles. Some time later, in the early twentieth century, Confederate memorial groups erected tributes to Stonewall Jackson and other Southern commanders. In 1940, the federal government established the site as a National Battlefield Park.

Known for his fervent religious devotion, General Stonewall Jackson maintained a strong religious atmosphere among his troops. Here, he leads his troops in a prayer.

RELATED SITES

GREELEY HOUSE

The New Castle Historical
   Society
100 King Street
Chappaqua, NY 10514
914-238-4666

Horace Greeley, the well-known Civil War-era editor of the *New York Tribune,* once lived in this Westchester County home. The building currently houses the museum of the New Castle Historical Society and contains various material relating to Greeley, the *New York Tribune,* and other nineteenth-century newspapers.

WINSLOW HOMER STUDIO

5 Winslow Homer Road
Prout's Neck, ME 04070
NHL

The American painter Winslow Homer worked as an illustrator for *Harper's Weekly* during the Civil War, producing numerous pictures of military life on the Virginia front. These wartime scenes also provided the inspiration for Homer's earliest paintings. This site was the artist's late nineteenth-century studio and contains numerous prints of his work. It stands at the end of a private, gated road and can only be reached by pedestrians and bicyclists.

National Museum of American Art and National Portrait Gallery (Old Patent Office Building)

Washington, D.C.

A Hospital for the Wounded Soldiers

Known as the "Angel of the Battlefield," the forty-year old Clara Barton (above) began her Civil War nursing career tending to wounded soldiers in the Patent Office building (below). It presented an impressive and imposing façade in nineteenth century Washington, D.C., even after a devastating postwar fire. After serving as a Civil War hospital, it was occasionally used for public functions.

Since 1854, Clara Barton had worked diligently at her rather uninspiring job as a copyist in the United States Patent Office. As one of four females employed by this office, the only government agency that had women on its staff, Barton had become proficient at preparing handwritten copies of thousands of government-authorized patent agreements. Despite the abuse she withstood from her fellow employees, who made insulting remarks regarding her unusual status as a relatively well-paid and unmarried woman worker, Barton stuck with her job for three years.

The Democratic victory in the 1856 Presidential election caused Barton, an outspoken Republican, to lose her post, but she was reinstated in December 1860, soon after Lincoln was elected President. The outbreak of the Civil War the following spring made Barton feel frustrated with her mundane copying tasks. Like many women, she longed to participate more actively and more directly in the Civil War, and felt especially concerned with the mounting casualty toll the war was producing.

By July 1861, soon after the first major military engagement at Bull Run, Barton began devoting her spare time to caring for wounded soldiers. She did not have to go far to minister to her patients. Many of the injured had

been brought to the top floor of the Patent Office building and were laid in the uncompleted lumber room upstairs on tables that, according to another nurse's description, had been "knocked together from pieces of the scaffolding."

When the Civil War began, Washington, D.C., like most American cities, found itself ill-prepared to accommodate the massive numbers of wounded, who would pass through the city in the next four years. Given its proximity to Virginia battlefields, Washington, D.C. in particular, would become the temporary home to large numbers of sick and injured men. To deal with this enormous influx, numerous buildings were pressed into service as makeshift hospitals.

In the early days of the war, explained one relief worker, "Any building was considered fit for a hospital." Various hotels, colleges, and churches made room for patients, as did numerous government sites, that included one section of the Capitol building, the south lawn of the White House. It also included one wing of the U.S. Patent Office, which served as hospital, morgue, and temporary barracks until March 1863.

When it opened its doors to Civil War victims in the summer of 1861, the Patent Office stood as one of the finest neoclassical buildings in America. Like other buildings designed in the Greek Revival style, the Patent Office, with its imposing columns and a facade that resembled the Greek temple the Parthenon, symbolized the young American nation's affinity with the democratic traditions of ancient Greece.

Under the supervision of Robert Mills—the architect of the Brockenbrough mansion—the first wing of the Patent Office building was completed in 1840. It became an exhibition center for various patented objects and historical artifacts that reflected the progressive and enterprising spirit of the new nation. Work continued through the 1850s on the massive, white marble building, then overseen by architect Thomas Walter. During Clara Barton's tenure as a copyist and the years when it doubled as both the Patent Office and a Civil War hospital, the building remained unfinished. It was finally completed in 1867.

Despite its elegant design and imposing style, the Patent Office was not a good hospital. It could never meet the needs and demands of its patients and, by present-day

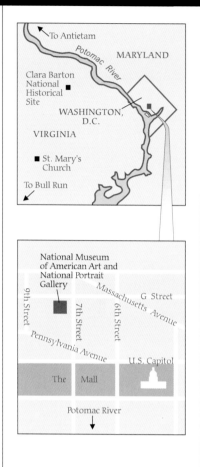

When it was constructed, the Patent Office building was hailed as a "temple to the industrial arts." Amidst the display cases showcasing various inventions, wounded Union soldiers received medical care in the cramped confines of the building.

The devastating wounds sustained by soldiers, as well as a fear of gangrene, frequently led army surgeons to amputate the limbs of wounded men. Many female nurses objected to amputations, believing that proper cleaning and treatment could help avoid this extreme surgical measure.

standards, the conditions were woefully inadequate and unsanitary.

Many beds were crammed together between the glass cases of the Patent Office artifacts. Used bandages were often strewn about the floor. One nurse described the clutter of objects and inventions in the improvised hospital ward as "a general nightmare of machinery." As such, the Patent Office hospital symbolized the primitive state of medical care in the early phase of the Civil War.

It also reflected Americans' optimistic faith that the war would be short, and therefore, their initial unwillingness to construct new and more permanent hospital facilities. It soon became apparent, however, that the war would not end quickly and that better hospitals would be required. By the fall of 1861, various officials and sanitary experts had begun to pressure the U.S. government to construct modern and more efficient hospitals in Washington, D.C., that could provide better ventilation and superior services for the sick and the wounded, who continued to flood the nation's capital.

Not only were the facilities inadequate, but the hospital personnel, especially nurses, had little training and insufficient medical knowledge to deal with the overwhelming amount of illness and injury produced by the war. New scientific advancements that revolutionized medical care in the 1860s, especially the knowledge of germs and sterilization, came too late for Civil War doctors. In addition, surgeons had few solutions, other than amputation, for treating severely wounded limbs.

In general, few hospital workers had an understanding of how diseases could spread, or how adequate nutrition might improve a patient's chance for survival. "Our hospitals," wrote one Union soldier, "are so bad that the men fight against being sent to them." Clara Barton had seen one young soldier who, despite having suffered from no more than an ordinary fever, almost died because army surgeons failed to provide him with adequate care and food. "His stockings," she observed, "had never been removed during all his illness and his toes were matted and grown together and are now dropping off at the joint, the cavities in his back are absolutely frightful."

Such conditions encouraged numerous women, especially in the North, to volunteer their services in the Civil War hospitals. They believed that by providing personal attention and oversight, they could help relieve the suffering and probably prevent the unnecessary deaths of many wounded men. Few women brought specific medical knowledge to their work. Nurses, both women and men, received no training since there was no nursing profession in 1861. Still, many women had considerable experience in caring for family members at home, and hoped to transfer that experience to the Civil War hospitals. At the very least, they could help soldiers write letters home or listen sympathetically to their worries and fears.

Some of the women, who found their way to the Patent Office hospital, had been recruited by Dorothea Dix, a sixty-year-old veteran of numerous reform crusades, who had recently been appointed to organize a female nurses' bureau in the U.S. Army. Others joined through the U.S. Sanitary Commission, a network of local support societies that had been initiated by women on the Northern homefront. Others, such as Clara Barton, worked on their own, apart from any organization.

Most women who worked in the Civil War hospitals did not come from the relatively privileged, middle-class background shared by Dix's nurses, U.S. Sanitary Commission women, and Clara Barton. The majority came from

Early in the war, some of the less capable soldiers, along with army musicians, served as stretcher-bearers, transporting wounded men from the field to waiting ambulances. By 1864, as one of the war's most significant medical innovations, a more efficient and well-trained ambulance corps was established in the Union army.

National Museum of American Art and National Portrait Gallery (Old Patent Office)

Eighth and F Streets
Washington, DC 20001
202-737-4215
www.npg.si.edu
www.americanart.si.edu

NRIS 66000902
NHL

DATE BUILT
1836–67

ARCHITECTS
Plans of the original architects, William P. Elliot and Ithiel Town, were modified during construction by Robert Mills. The building was completed by Thomas U. Walter.

SIGNIFICANCE
During the Civil War, the completed wings served as a hospital, a temporary barracks, and a morgue for Union soldiers. Abraham Lincoln's second inaugural ball was held here in March 1865. This Greek Revival building, the fourth federal building completed in Washington D.C., now houses the National Portrait Gallery and the National Museum of American Art.

the lower classes and performed jobs considered more menial than those done by nurses.

In Washington, D.C., many of the female hospital personnel were probably free blacks or former slaves. Throughout the South, slave women found themselves pressed into service on both sides of the conflict, working in Confederate hospitals for the wounded men of the South and caring for the Northern soldiers in Union army camps and hospitals. Some slave women no doubt welcomed the opportunity to work in this capacity for the Union cause, as it helped to secure liberation for themselves and their loved ones.

Susie King Taylor, a slave who had escaped to the Union army lines in occupied Georgia, worked as a laundress, teacher, and nurse for the Union soldiers, including many black soldiers. "I gave my services willingly for four years and three months without receiving a dollar," Taylor recalled in her postwar memoir. "I was glad, however, to be allowed to go with the regiment, to care for the sick and afflicted comrades."

Unlike the large numbers of African-American and Northern white women, who worked in the Civil War hospitals, Southern white women remained underrepresented in the wartime hospital corps. A few Confederate women took on significant responsibilities in Civil War medicine, some even became hospital supervisors. But most Southern ladies, complained one Confederate nurse, failed to "lend a helping hand," even "when there was such a wide field for every indispensable usefulness before them."

Many found the work undignified, especially given the social restrictions that Southern society placed on women working outside the home. Others yielded to the demands of male kin, who often refused to permit their women from engaging in what they considered unsuitable employment. In any event, Southern white women never provided a sufficient network of nurses and medical assistants that the Confederacy required. As a result, Confederate hospitals throughout the South generally suffered from a chronic lack of both staff and supplies.

Of course, women in neither the North nor the South monopolized Civil War nursing. Men, too, often served as nurses for disabled troops. Some were recuperating soldiers, recent patients in the hospital wards.

Others came from the civilian ranks. Perhaps the most famous of the Washington area nurses was the poet Walt Whitman. He often went to the Campbell and Armory Square hospitals and occasionally to the Patent Office. He came mainly to listen and offer emotional encouragement. "The doctors tell me," he wrote to a friend in 1863, "I supply the patients with a medicine which all their drugs & bottles & powders are helpless to yield."

And so, on the upper floor of what Whitman called the "noblest of Washington buildings," male and female nurses, along with army surgeons and other hospital personnel, did what they could amid the cramped conditions and exhibition cases to aid the wounded men. Using a system of pulleys, nurses and hospital workers managed to haul water, vegetables, and beef up the side of the building. By April 1862, At the urging of the U.S. Sanitary Commission, two modern facilities—Mount Pleasant and Judiciary Square hospitals—were completed. Improvements, at least in the Washington area, were introduced to Civil War medical care. The following spring, the Patent Office building ceased functioning as a hospital.

Clara Barton, in the meantime, had taken a leave of absence from her copying job, determined to play a more active, fulltime role in wartime nursing. No longer content to visit the wounded, who had been transported to Washington facilities, Barton now tended to men closer to the scenes of war, often on the fields of the battles. Her life and future work, including her founding of the American Red Cross in the 1880s, would be forever touched by her wartime nursing experiences. Her work also helped to open up the field of nursing as a new profession for women in the postwar years.

For the remainder of the war, the Patent Office Building functioned as it had before 1861, as a patent office for registering and showcasing new inventions and innovations. In March 1865, with the end of the Civil War just one month away, the grand and gaslit halls of the Patent Office building held President Lincoln's second inaugural ball.

The poet Walt Whitman spent three years nursing wounded soldiers in various hospitals around Washington, D.C., including those at the Patent Office. The experience greatly influenced Whitman's developing literary style.

The U.S. Sanitary Commission occupied this Richmond, Virginia building in 1865.

Twelve years later, in 1877, a fire decimated the exhibition halls in the north and west wings, destroying nearly 100,000 historic patent models. Viewed as a national calamity, the fire-ravaged sections were soon rebuilt, retaining most of the old design. The building continued to serve the needs of the Patent Office until 1932, at which time it became the headquarters, of the Civil Service Commission for the next thirty years. In 1958, the U.S. government transferred the building to the Smithsonian Institution, and in 1968 the building (presently also known as Old Patent Office Building) became the National Museum of American Art and the National Portrait Gallery.

RELATED SITES

BENTONVILLE BATTLEFIELD

5466 Harper House Road
Four Oaks, NC 27524
910-594-0789
http://www.ah.dcr.state.nc.us/
    sections/hs/bentonvi/
    bentonvi.htm
NHL

The battle of Bentonville, the largest to be fought in North Carolina, took place on March 19 to 21, 1865, and represented the best attempt by the Confederates to halt General William Sherman's

The private home of North Carolinian John Harper became a hospital during and after the battle of Bentonville.

march through the Carolinas in the spring of 1865. Used as a hospital site during the battle, the Harper House, a part of the state-owned Bentonville Battleground State Historic Site, is the only important building from the period still standing on the battlefield site. Today it houses exhibits on Civil War medicine. Some 554 soldiers, both Union and Confederate, were treated in this house that belonged to farmer and blacksmith John Harper.

ST. MARY'S CHURCH

5605 Vogue Road
Fairfax Station, VA 22032
703-978-4141
NHL

Now called St. Mary of Sorrows, this church, a simple one-story white frame building, was built by Irish immigrant railroad workers shortly before the Civil War. During the war, the building served as a field hospital in which Clara Barton worked

after the Battle of Second Manassas in August 1862. Union troops occupied the church and used the pews for firewood.

CLARA BARTON NATIONAL HISTORIC SITE

5801 Oxford Road
Glen Echo, MD 20812
301-492-6245
www.nps.gov/clba
NHL/NPS

This site, the post-Civil War home of Clara Barton, commemorates Barton's life and work. The building not only functioned as Barton's home after the Civil War, but also served as the headquarters and warehouse of the American Red Cross, founded by Barton in 1881.

Tannehill Furnace (Tannehill Ironworks Historical State Park)

near McCalla, Ala.

A Foundry for the Tools of War

Although relatively small in scale, the Tannehill Ironworks made a significant contribution to Confederate war production. The furnace, destroyed by Union troops at the end of the war, was recreated for the Tannehill Ironworks Historical State Park.

Few Civil War soldiers spent much time pondering the tools of their trade. Yet without question, their work could not have proceeded without certain essential implements, necessary for carrying out the tasks of war. Without guns and ammunition, there would have been no close combat; without cannons and cannon balls, no long-range assaults. And without skillets and pots, the Civil War soldier would have suffered from a lack of hot coffee and cooked food, although many, especially toward the end of the war, had to make do without these things anyway.

Many of these tools of war—instruments for both battle and camp—had to be manufactured in the relatively small workshops and factories that had sprung up throughout the United States in the first half of the nineteenth century.

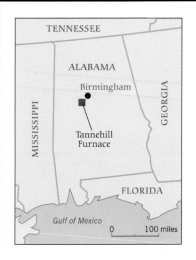

Most of these production sites were concentrated in the Northern states, as a part of the region's more developed system of manufacturing and industry. The South, in contrast, had long favored its agricultural sector over factory production. When the Civil War began, it was uncertain whether the Confederates would be able to produce the weapons needed to back up their convictions.

In 1861, at the outset of the war, a few factories could be found scattered through the Southern states. The largest and most significant foundry in the Confederacy was the Tredegar Iron Works in Richmond, Virginia. Incorporated in 1837, the Tredegar site eventually became the largest industrial complex south of the Potomac River, employing a workforce of nearly one thousand men. By the time of Virginia's secession in 1861, the Tredegar foundry was the only Southern facility with the capacity to produce major military supplies.

Elsewhere in the South, smaller iron workshops had sprung up in the prewar years, and some had the potential to become significant sites for war production. In the 1820s, in the western section of central Alabama on the banks of Roupes Creek, a Pennsylvania furnaceman Daniel Hillman constructed a forge for producing iron after discovering some extremely rich deposits of brown ore, or iron-bearing sediments. In 1844, Hillman's forge and the surrounding property was acquired by Ninion Tannehill. Although he was primarily a farmer, he eventually became the sole proprietor of the forge and made it a sideline to his agricultural operations.

Typical of Southern industry in the pre–Civil War years, the Tannehill Furnace conducted a fairly low-key business. Output was about 5 or 6 tons of iron a day. Workers cut wood from the surrounding pine forest and used it to make charcoal for firing the furnace. They dug ore from open pits and then hauled it, at first by hand and later along a tramway, two miles to the site of the forge. Here, the ore was melted and formed into shapes of crude iron, which in 1859 sold for $17.40 a ton.

From cutting the trees, to hauling the ore, to firing the furnace, all the work at Tannehill was done by slaves. Indeed, given the lack of an extensive free labor force, much of the South's industrialization in the prewar period was, by necessity, built on the backs of slave workers. During the 1850s, Southerners made their most noteworthy attempts to catch up with Northern manufacturing. They poured considerable money and energy into railroad production, textile mills, and iron workshops like those at Tannehill. In many of these sites, slaves were frequently the prime labor force.

Southerners' desire to industrialize, at least in the 1850s, was shaped by the intensifying political conflict. Many Southerners hoped that if more railroads, shoes, and clothes could be made in their own region, they would be less dependent on the North. Textiles seemed a particularly likely pursuit, given the huge amount of cotton grown in the South. By the early nineteenth century, Southern cotton was fueling an extensive textile industry in England as well as in New England. In the 1850s, the booming cotton economy led Southern planter and politician James Henry Hammond to proclaim, "Cotton is King." But as the decade drew to a close and war loomed, Yankees in the North continued to outpace Southerners in industrial output.

In 1860, despite Southern strides, the North had twice the railroad capabilities of the South and the South's share of national manufacturing actually declined from 18 to 16 percent. With agriculture, especially cotton yielding enormous profits, most Southerners, who had money to invest, preferred to put their cash into land and slaves rather than into iron or textile production. "To sell cotton in order to buy negroes, to make more

Plagued by a shortage of war materials, Southerners transformed domestic goods into military tools. Here, they are donating bells to cast into cannons.

cotton to buy more negroes," seemed to be the logic of Southern investing, explained one Northern observer.

Moreover, by the 1850s, many Southerners had come to believe in the superiority of an agrarian way of life and celebrated the advantages of rural living over the vice and decay associated with urbanization and manufacturing. This frequently led them to wax poetic about the beauties and benefits of plantation slavery over factory wage-labor. "Let the North enjoy their hireling labor," wrote the customs collector of Charleston, South Carolina, in the 1850s. "We do not want it. We are satisfied with our slave labor. . . . We like old things—old wine, old books, old friends, old and fixed relations between employer and employed."

However when war came, guns, cannons, and skillets were needed. The South had no choice but to press more slaves into industrial service. By 1863 at Tredegar Iron Works, the workforce had expanded to two thousand workers, half of whom were a combination of free and enslaved blacks. These workers churned out many of the Confederacy's weapons and artillery. They also forged the iron plate used by the famous ironclad ships first used in the Civil War.

After the Confederates seized the U.S. gunboat *Merrimack,* the iron plate, produced at Tredegar, helped remake it into the Confederate ironclad *Virginia.* When the armored *Virginia* met the Union's equally ironclad *Monitor* in a memorable duel at the mouth of the James River in

The Monitor *and the* Merrimack, *sketched here in a Union soldier's letter, heralded a new era in naval technology. The confederates transformed the captured* Merrimack *into the ironclad* Virginia *and set it against the* Monitor, *the first Union ironclad ship.*

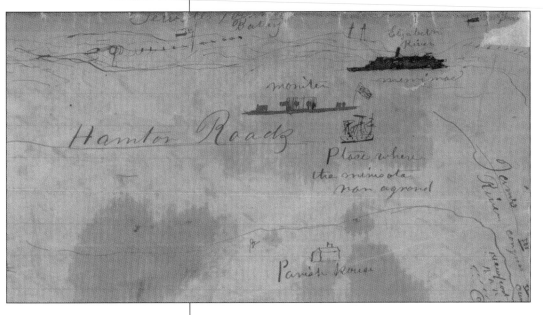

March 1862, naval warfare was forever transformed from a contest between graceful wooden ships into a grueling battle between hulking metal-sheathed vessels.

Perhaps the person most responsible for the Confederacy's ability to create the iron plate and other war products that were required by the army and the navy was Josiah Gorgas, the chief of the Ordnance Bureau. By providing lucrative government advances to firms that would convert to government production, Gorgas managed to obtain a staggering amount of weaponry and iron plate from the South's relatively weak factory system. At smaller establishments, like the one at Tannehill, Gorgas's policies made it possible for a minor workshop to become a significant site of war production.

In 1862, using a $50,000 advance in bonds issued by the Confederate government, Tannehill Furnace's new owner, William L. Sanders, built a second furnace and introduced a steam plant to replace the less reliable system of water power. Some of the expanded workforce at Tannehill came from the Confederate Army, but six hundred slaves continued to perform much of the work. A small tramway, which the remains are still visible, aided the workers in moving the ore to the furnace, in which the iron was heated and turned into a liquified mass.

Workers felled trees at a furious pace in order to keep the furnaces blasting continuously. Production increased considerably. Tannehill produced as much as 20 tons of iron a day, most of it used for cannon balls and gun barrels, as well as pots, pans, and skillets for Southern soldiers.

Despite the strides made by 1863, the Confederate war economy faced monumental obstacles toward the end of the conflict. Able to obtain higher prices on the open market, many manufacturers began to renege on government contracts. In many factories, machinery and spare parts became worn out. In addition, a blockade by the Union navy tried to prevent goods coming into or going out of the Confederacy. This made it difficult to obtain replacements.

A few factories went bankrupt when the Confederate government could not pay for its goods. And throughout the South, the lack of an effective railroad system made it difficult, sometimes impossible, to move raw materials to the factories and manufactured goods to the consumers.

Tannehill Furnace (Tannehill Ironworks Historical State Park)

12632 Confederate Parkway
McCalla, AL 35111
205-477-5711
www.tannehill.org

NRIS 72000182

DATE BUILT
1830

BUILDER
Daniel Hillman

SIGNIFICANCE
At the height of its production, Tannehill Furnace produced as much as 20 tons of iron a day. This iron was made into Confederate ordnance, cookware, and ovens. The factory employed six hundred slaves and was destroyed by a fire set by the Union army on March 31, 1865. The site now includes the Iron and Steel Museum, which explores the history of technology of the first half of the nineteenth century.

Tools of Destruction: The Minie Ball

Among the goods produced at the Tannehill Furnace were gun barrels for the weapons of the Confederate infantry. More specifically, the workers at Tannehill, and elsewhere in the North and the South, had begun to produce gun barrels that were rifled with spiral grooves cut into the interior surface, or bore.

Weapons manufacturers had long been aware of the superiority of rifled barrels. Compared to the older ungrooved, smooth-bore weapons, which did not create spin, the grooves caused bullets to spin through the air with increased range and accuracy.

Until the 1850s, however, rifled guns were used infrequently in warfare because of the extremely difficult and time-consuming process of getting a ball-shaped bullet down the rifled barrel. A soldier might spend precious minutes ramming the bullet down, and then several more minutes after a few firings cleaning out the residue of gunpowder that tended to accumulate in the grooves.

Then, in the 1850s, soldiers around the world began to use a new type of bullet that had been perfected by a French army captain named Claude E. Minie. Known as the minie ball, Minie's bullet was actually shaped more like a cylinder. It was slightly smaller than the rifle's bore and had a cone-shaped opening at its base which concentrated the force of the exploding gunpowder behind the bullet for greater power and a straighter path. Most important, it could be rammed down the rifled barrel easily and thus allowed a soldier to fire more quickly as well as more accurately.

In the United States, prior to the Civil War, Minie's bullet received further modifications and improvements. At the time of the war, weapons manufacturers in both the North and the South gradually made the switch from smoothbore guns to newer types of rifles that could accommodate the so-called minie ball.

Most historians have concluded that the switch had deadly consequences for Civil War soldiers. Although the new rifled weapons were far more accurate than the old guns, army leaders continued to rely on old tactical maneuvers. They continued to arrange their troops in a close-order formation to charge the enemy. But defending soldiers, armed with better rifles, could cripple such assaults.

As a result, the casualty rate on Civil War battlefields skyrocketed. Eventually, the Civil War commanders recognized the need for new tactics: advance by rushes in smaller groups and fight less on horseback and more on foot because a horse could be knocked down by an experienced riflemen. However, the change in tactics came slowly; and the price of using the new more effective rifles and bullets was paid by the hundreds of thousands of Northern and Southern men killed and wounded in battle.

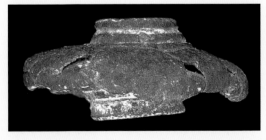

The lead minie ball, which could be fired much faster than older ammunition, changed the nature of Civil War fighting. These two minie balls collided head-on at the Battle of Fredericksburg, Virginia.

The region's rich cotton economy also suffered during the war. The Union's naval blockade prevented the South from trading cotton outside its borders. In addition, the Confederates themselves curtailed their cotton trade to the extent that they could slip past the blockade, in the hope that this might make foreign powers—especially Great Britian—feel the pinch of the declining cotton supplies.

Deprived of this essential product, Confederates reasoned, the British government might lend aid and recognition to the South. Unfortunately, this strategy of cotton diplomacy backfired. The diminished supply of cotton offered a much-needed incentive for the British economy to shift away from cotton textiles, which were saturating the world market, into more profitable industries such as iron and steel production.

More successful than many of the South's war production sites, Tannehill Furnace continued to produce huge quantities of guns, cannonballs, and army utensils until the very end of the conflict. At the end of March 1865, only a week or so before Robert E. Lee's final surrender at Appomattox Court House, three Iowa companies of Union soldiers marched on the Alabama furnaces and burned the trestles that suported the furnaces, the tramways, the cast houses, where liquefied iron was made into shapes, and the nearby settlement houses at Tannehill Furnace.

The two huge furnace stacks—tall structures attached to the furnaces that preheated the air—were spared from the blaze and resold at the end of 1865 to Tannehill's prewar owner, John Alexander. They were eventually acquired by the Republic Steel Corporation. Then in 1969, the University of Alabama deeded the sixty-six-acre preserve to a commission for the purpose of establishing a historical park. Today it is a state historic site, with an Iron and Steel Museum that displays early nineteenth-century technology.

The manufacturing firm of Cook and Brother, in Athens, Georgia, produced this and other .58 caliber carbines for use by Confederate soldiers.

LOWELL NATIONAL HISTORICAL PARK

246 Market Street
Lowell, MA 01852
978-970-5000
www.nps.gov/lowe
NPS

The town of Lowell was incorporated in 1826 and rapidly became the home of the high-volume, mechanized textile mills. During the Civil War, the fear of cotton shortages, which proved largely unfounded, caused many of the mills to close, throwing ten thousand people into unemployment.

SAUGUS IRON WORKS NATIONAL HISTORIC SITE

244 Central Street
Saugus, MA 01906
781-233-0050
www.nps.gov/sair
NPS

This is the site of the first integrated iron works in North America, dating to the period from 1646 to 1668. It includes a reconstructed blast furnace, forge, rolling mill, and a restored seventeenth-century house. Exhibits demonstrate the critical role of ironmaking in the lives of early New England settlers.

SLATER MILL HISTORIC SITE

67 Roosevelt Avenue
Pawtucket, RI 02862
401-725-8638
www.slatermill.org
NHL

Samuel Slater created America's first successful water-powered spinning machine in 1790 and opened the country's first successful cotton mill in 1793. Various establishments, mostly producing cotton, continued to operate in Slater's Mill during the Civil War years. The mill is now a museum.

TREDEGAR IRON WORKS

3215 West Broad Street
Richmond, VA 23223
804-226-1981
www.nps.gov/rich
NHL/NPS

Founded in 1837, the Tredegar Iron Works was one of the largest iron works in the United States until 1865. It supplied the South with a large share of the Confederacy's iron. Although the original Tredegar buildings are no longer standing, the visitors center for the Richmond National Battlefield Park is located in the Pattern Storage Building. It was once part of the Crenshaw Woolen Mills, which made blankets for the Confederate army, and then it became part of the Tredegar complex after the war.

The extensive and highly mechanized mills of Lowell, Massachusetts, symbolized Northern economic might in the years before the Civil War.

Port Hudson

Port Hudson, La.

A Sacred Ground for Emancipation

Captain André Cailloux was a superb horseman, a respected commander, and a recognized leader of his New Orleans community. Educated in Paris, Cailloux was fluent in both English and French. He was also a black man and, in fact, liked to refer to himself as the blackest man in New Orleans. Captain Cailloux had been raised in the free black community of New Orleans. He had acquired property and a position of stature, and when the Civil War came, he hoped to join the soldier ranks.

He raised a company of black troops—the First Louisiana Native Guards—many of whom, like Cailloux, came from some of the most prominent families of black New Orleans. Initially, the Louisiana Guards formed with the intention of serving the Confederate cause. The Confederacy, however, refused their services, and after Federal troops captured New Orleans in May 1862, Cailloux and his men joined forces with the Union.

A year later, Cailloux found himself in a position to lead his men into battle. On the morning of May 27, 1863, Captain Cailloux directed his troops in an extremely dangerous assault against a body of well-entrenched

After the fall of Vicksburg in July 1863, Union troops gained the momentum that ultimately allowed them to take possession of Port Hudson, the last Confederate outpost on the Mississippi River.

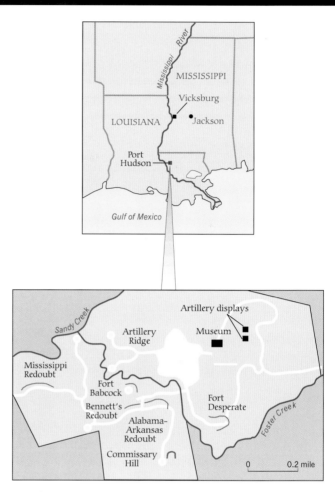

Confederates at Port Hudson, Louisiana, a town that lay seventeen miles north of Baton Rouge, along the Mississippi River.

Hoping to block a Union assault on New Orleans from the north, the Confederates had begun erecting fortifications at Port Hudson in early April 1862. Although New Orleans fell under Federal occupation a few weeks later, Port Hudson remained a key Confederate outpost on the Mississippi River. Indeed, as the Union stepped up its campaign to wrest complete control of the Mississippi River from Confederate hands, Port Hudson stood as a vital point in that campaign.

By the spring of 1863, Jefferson Davis's administration had pinpointed the steamboat-river-port town as the southernmost spot on a 230-mile stretch of the Mississippi River, which they intended to hold at all cost. The northernmost point of this stretch was Vicksburg, Mississippi, a city that was now under siege by General Ulysses S. Grant.

Grant's objective was to break the Confederates' hold on the Mississippi River, thereby severing this vital supply and transport line in the Southern states and effectively cutting the eastern portion of the Confederacy from the West. While Grant planned his assault against Vicksburg in the north, General Nathaniel Banks led his troops from the south in an attempt to dislodge the rebels from Port Hudson.

High on the bluffs overlooking the Mississippi River, Port Hudson—like Vicksburg to the north—presented daunting obstacles to the attacking Federal forces. One hundred years earlier, Spanish and French explorers had recognized the military significance of the site that would later become Port Hudson. Here, the Mississippi River narrows and then turns sharply below a steep bluff that rises seventy-five feet above the Mississippi River. The terrain, consisting of canyonlike ravines, high bluffs, and thick woodlands, is extremely rugged and at points nearly impenetrable. The high terrace situated above the Mississippi River gave the Confederates a natural plateau for their cannons, which could be aimed at any ships or troops coming from below.

In May 1863, the Union army, under the command of General Nathaniel Banks, had managed to secure a horseshoe-shaped position around the woefully under-manned Confederate fortifications. The 3,500 Louisiana, Arkansas, Mississippi, Alabama, and Tennessee troops positioned here hastily constructed a defense against the approaching Federal forces.

Among the thirty thousand soldiers in Banks's army were the First and Third Louisiana Native Guards (later to become the Seventy-third and Seventy-fifth Colored Infantry), some of the first black men to enlist in the

Union struggle. The First Louisiana Native Guards comprised of free black men of stature and prominence from the New Orleans community and in the prewar the Louisiana militia had comprised an all-black unit. The Third Louisiana Native Guards consisted of former slaves.

Confederate officials, who remained committed to fighting for black enslavement, refused the service of the First Louisiana Native Guards. That unit, as well as the Third, then lent their services to the Union commander Benjamin Butler in April 1862. They became part of the general's attempts to organize other African-American regiments with black officers—including both those with and without government commissions—into a "Corps d'Afrique," an African Corps.

Even in the Union, the services of Louisiana's black soldiers were not welcomed at first with wholehearted enthusiasm. The Lincoln administration remained reluctant to acknowledge and authorize regiments like the Louisiana Native Guards. The Civil War, as Lincoln and many in the Union high command defined it in 1862, was not a struggle against slavery but a fight to maintain national unity and stop secession. They viewed the conflict as "a white man's war" and refused to accept African Americans as soldiers in the fight.

By the end of 1862, however, the Federal government had begun to change the terms of the war, recognizing that the Union could not simply be restored as it had been but would have to be fundamentally altered. The Confederacy, the Union now maintained, could be broken only by destroying its fundamental institution of racial slavery.

As Lincoln gave more prominent attention to defeating slavery, he also became more interested in recruiting and utilizing the services of black troops. The Republicans

Broadsides, such as this one published by black abolitionist Frederick Douglass, appeared throughout the North after 1862, urging African-American men to enlist in the Union war effort. Spurred on by the Emancipation Proclamation, black men were eager to further the cause of slave liberation.

realized that former slaves and free blacks could help strike a devastating blow against the South. As a result, the Emancipation Proclamation, which took effect on January 1, 1863, declared slaves in the seceded states to be free and authorized the official enlistment of black soldiers into the Union army.

The measure, not surprisingly, was greeted with outrage by the Confederate government. Confederate army leaders declared their intention to kill any officer, white or black, who led African-American troops, claiming that such an officer perpetrated "crimes and outrages" against the Confederate citizenry, especially in inciting slaves to rebel. Black soldiers, particularly black prisoners of war, received extremely harsh treatment from Confederates in the field. Some were summarily executed.

Moreover, official acceptance into the Union army brought with it new burdens for African-American troops. They were routinely placed into segregated units, where they were paid several dollars a month less than whites and were obliged to take their orders from white officers. When General Banks assumed the leadership of the Louisiana forces, including the troops who made up the Native Guard units, he attempted to remove all African-American commanders.

In addition, the Union administration and the general Northern white public maintained considerable skepticism about the fighting capacities of black soldiers. Many accepted the idea that free blacks and former slaves might form labor battalions to build trenches and fortifications that would free white soldiers for active military duty. But most, including the white officers, who commanded the black troops, had to be convinced that African-American soldiers would not crack under fire.

The Port Hudson campaign was the first significant military engagement in the Civil War in which black troops saw active military service. There, the "experiment," as many whites termed it, of black military service was first tested. It was also one of the few battles in which black soldiers fought under black leadership, as the First Louisiana Native Guards had thus far managed to resist efforts to whiten its officer corps. The Guards came to Port Hudson with leaders, who included the esteemed Captain Cailloux and a young second lieutenant John Crowder.

Port Hudson

756 West Plains-Port Hudson
    Road
Zachary, LA 70791
504-654-0377
*www.cr.nps.gov/nr/travel/louisiana/
    por.htm*

NRIS 74002349
NHL

DATE OF BATTLE
1863

SIGNIFICANCE
Port Hudson was the final Confederate stronghold on the Mississippi River to fall to Union forces in July 1863. A Union attack on May 27, 1863, caused heavy losses to the First and Third Louisiana Native Guards. After the fall of Port Hudson, Arkansas, Texas, and most of Louisiana were separated from the rest of the Confederacy. Today, Civil War reenactments are held at this site.

The Heroism of the Massachusetts Fifty-fourth

Some two months after the May 1863 battle at Port Hudson, black soldiers again proved their abilities. They were from the Fifty-fourth Regiment, Massachusetts Volunteer Infantry, a unit that had attracted prominent African-American men from the North, including two sons of the abolitionist Frederick Douglass.

The governor of Massachusetts, John Andrew, had initiated this regiment to showcase black contributions to the war effort. He had handpicked the young and esteemed Robert Gould Shaw to be the regiment's commander. A committed white abolitionist, Shaw protested the unequal salaries imposed on black and white soldiers and urged the Union leadership to give his troops a chance to show their courage under fire.

On July 18, 1863, Colonel Shaw led his soldiers in a frontal attack on Fort Wagner, a Confederate earthwork that stood at the entrance to Charleston Harbor, South Carolina.

The superb defensive position of Fort Wagner gave the Confederates a great advantage against the Union troops. Shaw's regiment took the largest casualties, with Shaw receiving a fatal bullet wound to the chest. Nonetheless, his men pushed on and some even managed to penetrate the fort before the final Union retreat. When the battle ended, the Massachusetts Fifty-fourth Regiment had sustained a staggering casualty rate of over 40 percent.

Northern interest in Shaw and his regiment meant that national attention was riveted on the Fort Wagner battle. Again, Northern public opinion began to recognize the military fortitude of African-American soldiers. Fort Wagner, claimed the *New York Tribune,* would become "to the colored race as Bunker Hill had been for ninety years to the white Yankees."

The pride for the regiment, as well as a desire to memorialize the fallen troops and Shaw, spurred a monument that would pay tribute to the men of the Massachusetts Fifty-fourth Regiment and the attack on Fort Wagner.

Soon after the battle, some of the soldiers of the Fifty-fourth Regiment proposed a memorial to Colonel Shaw. In 1882, a committee of prominent Bostonians pushed the work forward and commissioned the sculptor Augustus St. Gaudens.

St. Gaudens depicted Shaw on horseback surrounded by his soldiers. He paid considerable attention to the individual soldiers and made careful likenesses of numerous black models. The final sculpture was hailed as a superb tribute to Shaw and his men and is considered by some to be one of America's finest public monuments.

Unveiled on Boston Common in 1897, the Shaw Memorial has offered an important focal point for Civil War memorialization. At the original unveiling, black and white dignitaries and veterans of the Massachusetts Fifty-fourth Regiment participated in a large public ceremony. In 1989, the movie *Glory* paid tribute to the story of Shaw and his men.

In 1997, at the one hundredth anniversary of the monument's unveiling, thousands gathered again to listen to the tributes to these Civil War troops. Over the years, many have visited the monument, where it remains opposite the Massachusetts State House. There, visitors learn about and pay their respects to the officers and soldiers of the Fifty-fourth Regiment of the Massachusetts Volunteer Infantry.

Some of the black soldiers of the Fifty-forth Regiment, Massachusetts Volunteer Infantry, in their daring attempt to capture Fort Wagner, managed to scale the walls and gain entry into the heavily-defended fortification. Northerners celebrated the soldiers' heroism, as well as the bravery of their white commanding officers.

Although born free like Cailloux, Crowder had come from a less fortunate background. Deserted by a father and a stepfather, Crowder had earned his own way since the age of eight. He had, however, managed to secure a decent education, and at sixteen became a lieutenant in Cailloux's company. He may have been the youngest officer in the Union army. "If Abraham Lincoln knew that a colored Lad of my age could command a company," Crowder once remarked to his mother, "what would he say?"

Crowder prepared himself and his men for the charge at Port Hudson. Surrounded by hills and embankments on one side and Foster Creek and Sandy Creek, as well as a series of ravines on the other, the Confederates occupied an extremely strong position. Moreover, the Confederates had positioned themselves on a bluff that ran next to the road that approaching troops would likely proceed along. The area between the bluff and the road was blocked with heavy underbrush and fallen trees.

On the morning of May 27, 1863, a column of white soldiers made the first assault, coming down the hills and embankments north of the Confederate defense.

A Black Journalist Recounts the War's End

Thomas Morris Chester's account of the prominent role played by black Union soldiers in the fall of Richmond at the end of the Civil War was published in the Philadelphia Press *in April 1865. Chester, the nation's only black correspondent during the Civil War, wrote this account in the hall, where the Confederate Congress had met.*

Seated in the Speaker's chair, so long dedicated to treason, but in the future to be consecrated to loyalty, I hasten to give a rapid sketch of the incidents which have occurred since my last dispatch...

Brevet Brigadier General Draper's brigade of colored troops, Brevet Major General Kautz's division, were the first infantry to enter Richmond. The gallant 36th U.S. Colored Troops, under Lieutenant Colonel B. F. Pratt, has the honor of being the first regiment.

In passing over the rebel works, we moved very cautiously in single file, for fear of exploding the innumerable torpedoes which were planted in front. So far as I can learn none has been exploded, and no one has been injured by those infernal machines. The soldiers were soon, under engineers, carefully digging them up and making the passage way beyond the fear of casualties.

Along the road which the troops marched, or rather double quicked, batches of negroes were gathered together testifying by unmistakable signs their delight at our coming. Rebel soldiers who had hid themselves when their army moved came out of the bushes, and gave themselves up as disgusted with the service....

These scenes all occurred at the terminus of Osborn road, which connects with the streets of the city, and is within the municipal limits. There General Draper's brigade, with the gallant 36th U.S.C.T.'s drum corps, played "Yankee Doodle" and "Shouting the Battle Cry of Freedom," amid the cheers of the boys and the white soldiers who filed by them. It ought to be stated that the officers of the white troops were anxious to be the first to enter the city with their organizations, and so far succeeded as to procure an order when about three miles, distant, that General Draper's brigade should take the left of the road, in order to allow those of the 24th Corps, under General Devin, to pass by. General Draper obeyed the order, and took the left of the road in order to let the troops of Devin go by, but at the same time ordered his brigade on a double-quick, well knowing that his men would not likely be over taken on the road by any soldiers in the army. For marching or fighting Draper's 1st Brigade, 1st division, 25th Corps, is not to be surpassed in the service, and the General honors it with a pride and a consciousness which inspire him to undertake cheerfully whatever may be committed to his execution. It was his brigade that nipped the flower of the Southern army, the Texas Brigade, under Gary, which never before last September knew defeat. There may be others who may claim the distinction of being the first to enter the city, but as I was ahead of every part of the force but the cavalry, which of necessity must lead the advance, I know whereof I affirm when I announce that General Draper's brigade was the first organization to enter the city limits. According to custom, it should constitute the provost guard of Richmond.

This first attack was quickly repulsed. Situated on the extreme right of the Union line, the black regiments then began to cross Foster's Creek by a pontoon bridge and made their way to the road, south of the creek. Hoping for back-up support from the Union artillery and white troops, the African-American soldiers gained little assistance after the Confederates had effectively silenced the supporting Union guns. Eventually, the African-American soldiers managed to emerge from the woods, and charged in the face of the concentrated strength of the Confederates' fire.

Despite heavy losses, the black troops reformed their lines and continued the attack. They regrouped and charged several times, mounting their casualty toll. At one point in the battle, a number of the Louisiana Native Guards even attempted to swim across a ditch that was intentionally created by the Confederates from the Mississippi River's backflow. It separated the advancing Union soldiers from the rebel line. The obstacles and the rapidly rising casualty rate in the black regiments, proved overwhelming.

In the end, the conflict resulted in 37 killed and 155 wounded, out of a total of 1,080 African-American troops. Among the dead were Captain Cailloux, who had died while urging his troops into battle. Lieutenant

General Nathaniel P. Banks (on the horse on the right) accepts the Confederate surrender of Port Hudson on July 8, 1863. The capture of Port Hudson gave the Union complete control of the Mississippi River.

By the end of the Civil War, more than 200,000 black men—including this unidentified solider—had served with the Union's armed forces.

John Crowder also died later the same day, after being critically wounded in the fight.

The Union had been defeated on that day at Port Hudson but black soldiers had achieved a bittersweet success. The battle represented a turning point for white opinions about African American's fighting capacities. Numerous white officers commended the black troops and claimed they no longer doubted the military contributions that these troops could offer to the fight. "The severe test to which they were subjected," reported General Banks, "and the determined manner in which they encountered the enemy, leaves upon my mind no doubt of their ultimate success." The reporters of the *New York Times* also applauded the courage of the African-American soldiers and thereby helped to change public opinion regarding the use of black troops. "It is no longer possible," the *New York Times* proclaimed, "to doubt the bravery and steadiness of the colored race, when rightly led."

African Americans needed no convincing of their soldiers' bravery. They mourned the losses from Port Hudson, but continued to support and sustain the struggle for which those men had sacrificed their lives. In late July 1863, thousands from the New Orleans black community turned out for the funeral of Captain Cailloux, whose body had lain on the field for six weeks after the battle.

Many of the mourners carried, or wore on their clothing, miniature American flags, making clear their support for a Union victory. For some local blacks, the site of the Port Hudson battlefield came to hold special significance as a place for memorializing the heroic contributions that had been made. One year after the battle, a white Union chaplain came upon a husband and wife, both former slaves, who sat upon the very spot where the black troops had fought. Holding their Bible, they read and reflected on the passage "I am the resurrection and the life."

Following the battle of May 27, Banks's army retreated and prepared for a renewed assault against the Confederates at Port Hudson. The second main attack came two weeks later, on June 14, but again the Confederates held their ground. At last, on July 4, 1863, General Ulysses Grant achieved his long-sought victory at Vicksburg, placing the Union in almost complete control of the Mississippi River. Grant, then, prepared to send a contingent of men south to finally remove the Confederates from the last strategic holdout on the river.

The news of Vicksburg's surrender was enough to convince the Southern forces, who remained at Port Hudson, that a continued fight would be fruitless. They realized that Confederate General Joseph Johnston, who had been recently defeated at Vicksburg, was in no position to assist them. By this point, their food supply had dwindled to mules and rats.

Thus, the final surrender of Port Hudson, on July 9 1863, signaled the complete return of the Mississippi River to Federal hands. "The Father of Waters," proclaimed Lincoln, "again goes unvexed to the sea." And while Captain Cailloux did not live to see this victory, he and his men had helped lay the groundwork for this crucial turning point in the Civil War.

Today, there are 640 acres of the historic battlefield, which are maintained by the state of Louisiana as a State Commemorative Area.

FORT PILLOW HISTORIC PARK

Route 2, Box 109-A
Henning, TN 38041
731-738-5581
*www.state.tn.us/environment/
    parks/pillow/*
NHL

Confederate engineers constructed this fort, but Union
troops occupied it in June
1862. It was recaptured in
April 1864 by Confederate
forces under Major General
Nathan Bedford Forrest. Of
the 262 black Union soldiers,
who fought alongside 310
white compatriots, 229 died.
They were mostly ex-slaves,
who had been recruited in
Tennessee and Alabama. The
original earthworks have
been preserved. At present,
the site is a wildlife refuge.

RICHMOND NATIONAL BATTLEFIELD PARK

3215 E Broad Street
Richmond, VA 23223
804-226-1981
www.nps.gov/rich
NPS

Among the numerous battle
sites that are part of this park
is the site of a September 29,
1864, assault by fourteen
African-American regiments,
most of them from the United
States Colored Troops, on a
Confederate fortification at
New Market Heights,
Virginia. Fourteen of these
soldiers who participated in
this assault were awarded the
Medal of Honor. They com-
prised fourteen of the sixteen
black Medal of Honor recipi-
ents from the entire Civil War.

ROBERT GOULD SHAW AND THE FIFTY-FOURTH REGIMENT MEMORIAL, BOSTON AFRICAN AMERICAN NATIONAL HISTORIC SITE

Boston Common
Beacon and Park Streets
Boston, MA
www.nps.gov/boaf/site1.htm
NPS

A fund started by a former
slave Joshua B. Smith in 1865
helped create a bronze
statue to commemorate the
black infantry unit designated
the Fifty-fourth Regiment,
Massachusetts Volunteer
Infantry. The unit, with its
commander Robert Gould
Shaw, led the assault on Fort
Wagner on July 18, 1863. The
attack led to the first time a
black man, Sergeant William
Carney, was awarded the
Congressional Medal of
Honor.

Gettysburg National Military Park

Gettysburg, Pa.

The War at a Turning Point

Although Confederate General George Pickett would have his name forever linked with the Confederate offensive that closed the Battle of Gettysburg, Pickett's superior, General James Long-street, actually coordinated the assault. Numerous artists and writers, including William Faulkner, would later draw inspiration from this famous charge.

In June 1863, Confederate commander Robert E. Lee prepared to move the Civil War in an entirely new direction. With Union General Ulysses S. Grant gathering his forces in the west for a concerted siege against Vicksburg, Mississippi, Lee thought an offensive push in the east might force the Union army to ease up on the Vicksburg campaign.

As he had done once before, Lee planned to move the war out of the South and into enemy territory to demonstrate the Confederates' military might in Lincoln's backyard. Such a victory, he believed, would signal to the world and to the Union administration the futility of prolonging the war against the South, now entering its third year. Lee hoped that then the Republican government, would be forced to negotiate with the South and end the war in Confederates' favor.

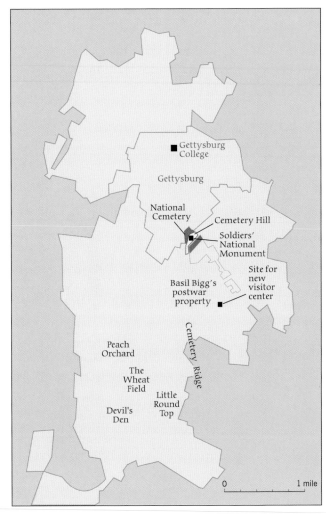

Given Lee's amazing string of military successes, and his troops' apparent invincibility, Confederate President Jefferson Davis agreed that priority should be given to this daring initiative.

Lee's plans took shape in the form of a Confederate campaign into Pennsylvania, eventually culminating in what would be the bloodiest battle of the Civil War and the largest battle ever to occur in the Western Hemisphere. The fate of the nation would be altered by the fighting that occurred on the hills and in the fields that lay just outside the town of Gettysburg, a relatively tranquil farming community and a small college town. The town and the surrounding landscape would likewise be irrevocably altered, as would the lives of the men and women who lived there and those who participated in the battle. The battlefield at Gettysburg would become one of the nation's most important landmarks.

With his army well rested and well supplied and morale among Southern troops and civilians at a high point, Lee sensed that the time was right to begin his Northern assault. In mid-June 1863, he moved his army of seventy-five thousand men through Virginia's Shenandoah Valley and into south-central Pennsylvania. His troops were strung out from Chambersburg in the west to York in the east. Along the way, they gathered supplies and food from the countryside and seized local black residents, who were taken to the South to be enslaved. Lee wished to avoid acts of plunder to win the support of anti-Lincoln Northerners, but the troops did not always obey.

In the meantime, the ninety thousand men of the Union's Army of the Potomac followed in quick pursuit. They were led by General George Meade, the latest in a string of military leaders for the Union's main army in the east. Fearing that Meade might attack his dispersed troops, Lee gathered his men for a battle east of the mountains in the Gettysburg-Cashtown vicinity. Although the town of Gettysburg itself was small with only 2,400 inhabitants, it lay at the center of numerous roads that emerged from the surrounding mountains and valleys. By the end of June, both armies found themselves headed down those roads that converged upon this tiny hamlet.

As they marched toward Gettysburg, the soldiers passed through a gently rolling terrain, broken occasionally by scattered granite outcroppings. The town was home to a theological seminary and Gettysburg College. On the outskirts, it was surrounded by farmland—cultivated fields, orchards, and woodlots—that provided most of the region's inhabitants the basis for their livelihood. Among those who had come to work the land near Gettysburg was a small population of free black farmers. Hoping to make use of the agricultural possibilities in the countryside, they also came for the educational opportunities that the town of Gettysburg could offer their children.

One of the free black residents was Basil Biggs, a former Baltimore teamster and then a forty-four-year-old tenant farmer, who worked on the John Crawford homestead. Biggs had lived in Gettysburg since 1858. Having been active in the prewar struggle against slavery, he had occasionally hidden escaped slaves on the

Gettysburg National Military Park

97 Taneytown Road
Gettysburg, PA 17325
717-334-1124
www.nps.gov/gett

NRIS 66000642
NPS

DATE OF BATTLE
1863

SIGNIFICANCE
One of the decisive battles of the Civil War took place here from July 1 through 3, 1863. Union forces under General George Meade faced down the Confederate troops commanded by General Robert E. Lee. The Union forces held the hills, despite the heroic Confederate Pickett's charge on the last day of the battle. After this loss in the Union territory, the Confederates could not mount a successful offense. The fifty-one thousand casualties made Gettysburg the bloodiest battle in the war.

Crawford place. Then, in June 1863, Biggs got word of the approaching invasion. He probably also heard about the fate of the other Pennsylvania blacks, who had been kidnapped by Southern soldiers in the town of Chambersburg. Anxious to keep his own family safe, Biggs took his wife and four children to a neighboring community before the Confederate soldiers reached Gettysburg. He then returned to the town by himself, on July 1, the day the battle of Gettysburg began.

Fighting erupted in Gettysburg before even Lee had arrived on the scene. The Confederate commander had not intended to make a stand at this particular spot, but as the armies began to congregate to the north and northwest of the town, fighting gradually escalated. By the evening of July 1, at the end of the first day of the battle, the Confederate soldiers had managed to dislodge the Union troops from their initial positions outside the town. They had sent the Union soldiers running through the streets and onto the high ridge known as Cemetery Hill, a half-mile south of Gettysburg.

Lee, who had arrived by the afternoon, hoped to capitalize on his soldiers' morale and energy. He aimed to destroy, quickly and decisively, the Union soldiers,

Abraham Lincoln came to Gettysburg on November 19, 1863 to help dedicate the new national cemetery that had been created on the battlefield. He gave a two-minute speech that became one of the most admired orations in American history.

who had gathered on the southern ridge. His statement, "The enemy is there, and I am going to attack him there," was later recalled by his second in command, General James Longstreet. Lee ordered Longstreet to launch the main attack against the Union army's left flank as early as possible on the following day of July 2.

Longstreet, however, had misgivings about Lee's plans and did not begin his assault until late in the afternoon of the appointed day. He led his troops forward, into some of the war's deadliest fighting, onto sites that would become well known to thousands of veterans and their descendants in the years to come.

Soldiers in blue and gray fought one another fiercely that afternoon in spots below the Cemetery Ridge that would thereafter be known simply as the Peach Orchard and the Wheat Field. Blood was also shed in a maze of boulders called Devil's Den, as well as on a high hill at the extreme Union left, known to all as Little Round Top.

Thanks to quick thinking, coordinated maneuvering, and unparalleled bravery, the Union army managed to repulse the Confederate assault on the second day of battle. The costs were high. Each side had more than nine thousand casualties on this one day of fighting.

Still, Lee remained determined to achieve the victory he had come for. His faith in his troops remained unbroken. He believed they could, as they had often done before, accomplish what to others seemed impossible. But Lee, then fifty-six years old, was not in top form. The previous March, he had begun to show signs of a debilitating heart ailment that would cause his death a few years after the war. At Gettysburg, he was tired and

A Confederate Captain Writes about Gettysburg

 In a letter to his father, Confederate Captain George Hillyer of the Ninth Georgia Regiment described being in the thick of the battle at Gettysburg.

JULY 11TH, AT SUNDOWN

MY DEAR FATHER

The army is at this time encamped in the line of battle stretching away from the Potomac river to and beyond Hagerstown, expecting and preparing for an attack from the enemy. . . .

At the battle of Gettysburg, where Longstreet's corps was engaged on the 2d, our division, (Hood's) began the attack. . . . For nearly an hour the enemy were on three sides of us, and a battery of sixteen guns enfilading us with grape [grapeshot]. If it had not been for the shelter of rocks and trees behind which we fought, not one of us would have escaped. I changed the front of the three left companies so as to face the enemy every way, and we held the enemy at bay until the flank was relieved by the coming up of McLaws' division. . . . It was now nearly sundown. But simultaneously from all along our line, there went up a yell only such as our army can give when rushing on the foe. True, we were wearied and exhausted, and our ranks were thinned by the long contest, but we went forward as fast as we could. . . . I saw the cannon belching forth volumes of smoke all along the summit, but heard no report from them—the roar of musketry and the shouts of our men drowned every other sound. We did not pause or hesitate a moment, but advanced after emerging from the timber one or two hundred yards. . . . During this charge, I saw our men falling large numbers, and the enemy's infantry who were retreating before us, suffered very heavily, par-

ticularly as they went up the hill. I saw the ground ploughed and torn by grape shot and shell . . . but when we got to the foot of it and saw how steep it was, and how high it was, and how much our ranks were thinned, all seemed at once to perceive that the desperate effort must fail, and we turned and retired to a selected line in the woods. . . . The next day, in the battle of Friday, we were detached and fought the enemy's cavalry. . . . Of the position and events in front of Ewell and A. P. Hill, I know little more than you do. . . . Our wounded, except the few who were too badly hurt to be moved, we had brought off and cared for. Poor Jack Giles (I know how much you respected and esteemed his father) had his leg torn off by a shell just before we began to advance. He was about ten steps from me at the time, I went to him, and at once saw by his countenance and his extreme prostration, that he would die. I asked him what I must tell his father and his mother, in case I should live to see them. Shells were tearing the trees and the ground around us, but the heroism of his spirit triumphed even in that dreadful hour. His reply was simple and calm—"Capt. tell my father and my mother I died for my country."

I wonder somebody don't take to puffing the 9th regiment. It is one of the best and steadiest on the continent. But no pains having been taken to noise it in the newspapers, I suppose people at home know very little about it.

AFFECTIONATELY, YOUR SON,

GEORGE HILLYER

physically debilitated and may not have fully grasped the hopelessness of his position.

And so, on July 3, Lee ordered a final assault at the very center of the Union line, a frontal attack through the wheat field and up Cemetery Ridge. With great trepidation, Longstreet carried out Lee's order. At 1 P. M. that afternoon, the Confederates began the assault with a fierce bombardment against the Union artillery. But the Confederates' aim was too high and actually inflicted little damage on the Union forces.

Two hours later, the Confederate troops rushed forward, led by the flamboyant General George Pickett. One hour later, Pickett's charge had been crushed. Nearly half of the fourteen thousand soldiers who had set out in the valiant Confederate assault never returned. Only a small number ever breached the Union position.

Lee, recognizing the disastrous consequences of his plan, accepted full responsibility for the loss. Lee's aides, and a British war correspondent, recalled his words of regret when the battle had concluded. "It's all my fault," he told his men as he rallied them for the retreat back to Virginia.

Robert E. Lee was a changed man after the defeat at Gettysburg. He would go on to win continued military success during the next two years of the war. But he and his army would never again have the strength and

Some of the most moving pictures of the Civil War came in the aftermath of the Battle of Gettysburg when photographers such as Timothy O'Sullivan captured startling portraits of the six thousand men who died.

Gettysburg National Cemetery

Just as the battle that took place on the hills and wheat fields of Gettysburg represents a significant turning point in the military progress of the Civil War, so does President Lincoln's speech at the Gettysburg National Cemetery created four months after the battle. It represents a significant turning point in how the war was understood, especially by those who supported and fought for the Union.

In November 1863, the Gettysburg Cemetery Commission invited Lincoln to attend the dedication of this burial site. He planned to use the opportunity to offer a far-reaching statement on the meaning and significance of the Civil War. The ten-sentence address that Lincoln delivered at this solemn occasion became one of the most well-known speeches in American history.

Following two-and-a-half years of bloody Civil War, the fresh earthen mounds of the cemetery, where the bodies of thousands of soldiers who had fought in the war's bloodiest battle lay, offered the appropriate setting for Lincoln's sober and thoughtful reflections on why so much death and bloodshed had been necessary.

Although the cemetery would not be completed until 1872, landscape architect William Saunders had begun the planning and layout of the burial grounds. Lincoln summoned Saunders to the White House in order to learn more about the topography of the site, where he would give his speech.

During the dedication ceremony on November 19, 1863, Lincoln rose and delivered his Gettysburg Address (see page 92). In his brief oration, Lincoln explained that the war was fought not simply to save American liberties and Republican government, but to further the commitment to equal rights for

Landscape architect William Saunders emphasized a relatively sparse design, with wide, open lawn spaces, for the National Cemetery at Gettysburg. "The prevailing expression of the cemetery," explained Saunders, "should be that of simple grandeur."

all men, regardless of race, to bring forth "a new birth of freedom."

Moreover, he linked the commitment to equality with the promotion of more than just a union of the states, but a new and more powerful nation. "We here highly resolve," Lincoln said at the close,

> that these dead shall not have died in vain, that this nation, under God, shall have a new birth of freedom, and that government of the people, by the people, for the people, shall not perish from the earth.

In the North, people hailed the speech as one of the most inspiring and important orations of their era. Lincoln's words became forever tied to the consecrated ground of the Gettysburg National Cemetery.

Following the Civil War, the Gettysburg National Cemetery became a burial site for American veterans from other major wars and conflicts. Although now closed to new burials, it has also become the site for various monuments and memorials that pay tribute to the soldiers buried there.

prestige, which they had on the eve of the Gettysburg campaign. He would not again attempt an invasion of the North and from this point on would fight a more cautious and defensive war against the Union.

The events in Pennsylvania represented more than just a personal failure for Robert E. Lee. Not only had his plan to invade the North been defeated, but his goal of taking pressure away from the Vicksburg campaign had also failed. On July 4, the day after Lee's loss in Pennsylvania, news arrived of Grant's triumph at Vicksburg. With the Confederate surrender of this critical Mississippi stronghold and the subsequent loss of Port Hudson, the Union army was able to sever the South in two, cutting off the men and the supplies in the southwest from the struggling armies in the east.

Unquestionably, this double defeat firmly crushed any chance, still hoped for by Lee and Jefferson Davis on the eve of the Pennsylvania invasion, for support and recognition from Europe. Although the war did not end in July 1863, the twin calamities at Vicksburg and at Gettysburg dealt an overwhelming blow to the Confederate war effort.

Life changed for Basil Biggs, too, following the Gettysburg campaign. Recognizing how dangerous it was to be alone, an African-American man in the midst of this fierce battle, Biggs had kept himself hidden during the days of fighting. While he remained secluded, the farm on which he worked was virtually destroyed. Throughout the fighting, the Crawford farm had served as a vast Confederate hospital, where numerous casualties were treated and many of the dead were buried. In addition, a tremendous amount of food, crops, and household goods were either destroyed or taken, including 45 acres of wheat, 24 acres of corn, 8 milk cows, 7 steers, 10 hogs, 26 yards of carpeting, 16 chairs, and 2 sets of dishes.

In the years after the war, Biggs would file damage claims with both the state of Pennsylvania and the federal government, attesting to how much he had lost during those three days in July. Although the state agreed to pay $1,300 of Biggs's claim, the legislature never voted to provide the money. And, as far as records show, neither did the federal government offer any compensation. The battle of Gettysburg brought Basil Biggs's days as a tenant farmer on the Crawford farm to an end.

The Gettysburg Address

Abraham Lincoln spoke these words on November 19, 1863, at the dedication of the Gettysburg National Cemetery. Lincoln eloquently summarized the changed meaning of the Civil War. It is considered one of the greatest speeches in American history.

Fourscore and seven years ago our fathers brought forth on this continent a new nation, conceived in liberty, and dedicated to the proposition that all men are created equal.

Now we are engaged in a great civil war, testing whether that nation, or any nation so conceived, and so dedicated, can long endure. We are met on a great battlefield of that war. We have come to dedicate a portion of that field as a final resting-place for those who here gave their lives that that nation might live. It is altogether fitting and proper that we should do this.

But, in a larger sense, we cannot dedicate—we cannot consecrate—we cannot hallow—this ground. The brave men, living and dead, who struggled here, have consecrated it far above our poor power to add or detract. The world will little note nor long remember what we say here, but it can never forget what they did here. It is for us, the living, rather, to be dedicated here to the unfinished work which they who fought here have thus far so nobly advanced. It is rather for us to be here dedicated to the great task remaining before us—that from these honored dead we take increased devotion to that cause for which they gave the last full measure of devotion; that we here highly resolve that these dead shall not have died in vain; that this nation, under God, shall have a new birth of freedom; and that government of the people, by the people, for the people, shall not perish from the earth.

Because Lincoln's speech was so brief, the photographer who took this picture did not have time to take the President's portrait before he sat down. Lincoln is seen with his head inclined down without his characteristic top hat.

But in other ways, the battle of Gettysburg opened up new opportunities for Biggs. In October 1863, three months after the battle, he was hired as a teamster to assist in the removal of the Union dead to the newly created national cemetery there. While the fighting continued in places farther south, he carefully disinterred bodies, found in various states of decomposition, from the battlefield and hospital sites. He worked steadily and diligently at this gruesome task for the next five months, using a two-horse team, which allowed him to haul nine bodies at a time.

When the war ended, Biggs's service for the Union dead apparently marked him as a person of stature in the African-American community, allowing him to become an officer in a local black veterans' organization, the only nonveteran to do so. By the end of the war, Biggs had also become a property owner, having received a tract of land from the estate of another local black resident. Between 1865 and 1894, Basil Biggs lived his life as a farm owner and veterinarian, residing on a plot of land on the Taneytown Road, close to where the commanding Union General George Meade had made his headquarters during those momentous days in July 1863.

The battlefield became the site of intense memorialization and national remembrance soon after the battle had subsided. President Lincoln enshrined the ideals of Gettysburg upon the national memory when he delivered, in November 1863, his Gettysburg Address. Less than a year after the battle, the Gettysburg Battlefield Memorial Association had formed and acquired large tracts of battlefield terrain to preserve the site and memorialize the Union troops and officers who had fought there.

Throughout the late nineteenth century, Union veterans and memorial associations transformed the battleground with clusters of tablets, monuments, and statues to pay tribute to Northern soldiers. In 1895, the association's holdings, as well as land once owned by Basil Biggs, passed into the hands of the federal government.

In light of a burgeoning atmosphere of reconciliation and renewed nationalism, the federal government felt compelled to incorporate the Confederates' point of view into the Gettysburg landscape. In the early years of the twentieth century, Southern states were encouraged to erect monuments and memorials to their Civil War participants. Virginia's statue of Robert E. Lee was the

Over the years, the goal of preserving the battlefield has often clashed with commercial objectives, prompting continued discussion about the meaning of this critical location in American culture. Most recently, the National Park Service, which continues to maintain Gettysburg National Military Park, has undertaken an ambitious effort to restore many features of the 1863 landscape to the present battlefield site. The work has included the removal of an immense tourist observation tower.

Almost 150 years later, much of the historic battlefield landscape has remained intact, including numerous dips and ridges that once slowed the progress of advancing troops, and boulder clusters where sharpshooters nestled and took aim at enemy soldiers. Visitors today can immerse themselves in large portions of the Gettysburg landscape and get a remarkable sense of what the soldiers of 1863 must have seen.

The National Park Service has begun an ambitious plan to preserve and restore the landscape at Gettysburg.

GETTYSBURG BATTLEFIELD HISTORIC DISTRICT

Gettysburg, PA 17325
For more information on this
site contact:
State Historic Preservation
Office Bureau for Historic
Preservation Commonwealth
Keysone Building, 2nd Floor
400 North Street
Harrisburg, PA 17120-0093
717-787-2891
NHL/NPS

The Gettysburg Battlefield
Historic District includes
the boundaries of the
Gettysburg Military Park and
the Gettysburg National
Cemetery, where Lincoln gave
his address in 1863. It also
includes the town of
Gettysburg, where parts of
the battle took place and
where many of the wounded
were nursed in local churches. Also included is the
Eisenhower National Historic
Site-the site of the farm
owned by President and
Mrs. Dwight Eisenhower.

VICKSBURG NATIONAL MILITARY PARK

3201 Clay Street
Vicksburg, MS 39180
601-636-0583
www.nps.gov/vick
NPS

It took a nine-month cam-
paign for General Grant to
capture this Confederate
stronghold on the Mississippi
River. After a final forty-seven-
day siege, the city surrendered
on July 4, 1863, the day after
the Union victory was secured
at Gettysburg. Once Vicksburg
fell, Union troops were able to
seize Port Hudson, the last
Confederate outpost on the
Mississippi, with relative
speed. Thus, the victory at
Vicksburg represented a turning point in that it gave the
federal government complete
control of the Mississippi
River, effectively cutting the
Confederacy in two. The current site houses a reconstructed *USS Cairo* (below), a gunboat sunk by a mine. A six-
teen-mile drive takes one
along the Union siege line and
the Confederate defenses.

ANTIETAM NATIONAL BATTLEFIELD

PO Box 158
Sharpsburg, MD 21782
301-432-5124
www.nps.gov/anti
NPS

The battle at Antietam was
the bloodiest single day of
the Civil War and cost more
than twenty-three thousand
casualties on September 17,
1862. It also represented the
culmination of Lee's first
attempt—before the
Gettysburg campaign—
to invade the Northern states.
The Union's ability to stop
this first Confederate invasion
represented an important
turning point in the Civil War.
This Union victory provided
the impetus for Lincoln to
make public his Emancipation
Proclamation, which declared
the slaves in the seceded
states free. The current site
includes an eight-and-a-half-
mile driving tour route and
a small museum.

Honey Springs Battlefield

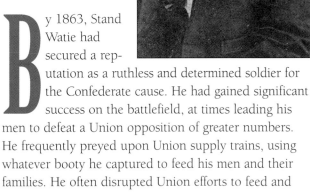

Checotah, Okla.

A Native American Battleground

Stand Watie (above) was a Cherokee leader and, by 1864, a Confederate brigadier general. The Battle of Honey Springs (below) was captured soon after by illustrator James O'Neill for the widely-read Leslie's Illustrated Newspaper.

By 1863, Stand Watie had secured a reputation as a ruthless and determined soldier for the Confederate cause. He had gained significant success on the battlefield, at times leading his men to defeat a Union opposition of greater numbers. He frequently preyed upon Union supply trains, using whatever booty he captured to feed his men and their families. He often disrupted Union efforts to feed and supply loyal Indians in Kansas.

Watie was a leader of the Cherokee Indian Nation, a significant landholder, and the owner of numerous black slaves. His commitment to the Confederacy not only reflected long-standing ties with Southern customs and

people, it also provoked a wider split within the American Indian community and within his own Cherokee Nation.

About twenty thousand Native Americans participated in the Civil War, fighting on both the Union and the Confederate sides of the conflict. They were active in numerous battles, including Second Bull Run in Virginia, Pea Ridge in Arkansas, and Chatanooga in Tennessee. A noted Seneca leader, Ely S. Parker, served as Ulysses Grant's military secretary throughout the war. Perhaps most significant Native American contributions to the war effort were in the so-called Indian Territory in the western frontier region, now present-day Oklahoma.

Many eastern tribes had been relocated to this region in the prewar years. The federal government had given them land there in exchange for their previous territories in the Southeast. Here, the actions and allegiances adopted by Native Americans in the Civil War were shaped largely by the tragic experiences of the preceding thirty years, and especially by the decision of the U.S. government in the 1830s to move Indians from their tribal lands in the east to unorganized public lands in the west.

This government policy set the basis for the "Trail of Tears," a forced relocation of several Native American tribes. Moving on foot and horseback the journey resulted in the death, demoralization, and impoverishment of tens of thousands of Indians.

Most affected by the relocation were the so-called Civilized Tribes of the Southeast, including the Creeks, the Choctaws, and the Cherokees. They were forced onto the new land that lay west of the Mississippi River. These Native American groups had given up numerous tribal customs and agricultural practices in favor of a system that more closely resembled American patterns of family farming. Yet, despite these adaptations, government officials believed that white Americans were more deserving of the land these tribes occupied.

Some Indian tribes even followed the Southern practice of owning black slaves. The removal policies and the decision to comply with U.S. government directives greatly weakened the Native American community, creating rifts not only between the tribes but also within them. For example, the Cherokees were divided between those who followed Stand Watie, a forceful advocate for removal and a strong proponent of slavery, and those who allied themselves with John Ross, an opponent of

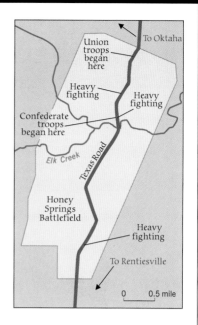

Begun as a missionary school for Native Americans, the Armstrong Academy in Oklahoma served as the capital for the Choctaws during the Civil War.

Indian relocation and, after 1846, Principal Chief of the Cherokee Nation. Although Ross himself owned several slaves, many of his supporters rejected Cherokee slaveholding practices and became advocates of abolition.

The Creeks, too, were split between Chief Opothleyahola, who had opposed the relocation of the tribes, and the members of the influential and powerful McIntosh family, who had urged compliance with government orders. The Civil War reignited these internal feuds, producing heated and violent confrontations within the western Indian tribes.

In the spring of 1861, the Confederate government sent Albert Pike, a frontier lawyer and former journalist, to the West to serve as a commissioner to the various tribes in the Indian Territory. The hope was to secure Native-American allies for the Confederate cause and to convince the tribes to sign new treaties with the Confederate government. Many Native Americans welcomed Pike and supported his efforts, believing they stood a better chance of protecting their land with the Confederates than they had with the Federal government in Washington D.C.

Many also felt certain affinities for the South, especially in the commitment to slavery. The Choctaw Nation, the first tribe to declare for the Confederate cause, proclaimed an indissoluble bond between their tribe and "the destiny of our neighbors and brethren of the Southern states." By the fall of 1861, the Creeks, the Seminoles, and the Choctaws had all signed treaties with the Confederate government.

Pressured by Watie and his Confederate sympathizers, John Ross, too, signed a treaty pledging Cherokee support for the Confederacy, although he felt a greater personal allegiance to the Union than to the Confederacy. In the meantime, many Unionist Indians, angered by the cooperation with the Confederacy, moved to Kansas and joined forces with the Union army, making up the First, Second, and Third Home Guards.

By the spring of 1862, many Cherokee troops had likewise switched their allegiance to the Union side and joined forces with the Kansas Home Guards. A few months later John Ross also declared his loyalty for the Union.

Watie remained the main Confederate supporter among the Cherokees. In October 1861, he was appointed a colonel in the Confederate army, charged with protecting the Indian Territory from Union invasion. Although he was a determined soldier, he was not a thoroughly satisfied ally of the Confederate effort. In letters to the Confederate government he criticized the South for making "no vigorous effort" to stop the Union forces in his region, and complained of the "incapable and slothful" Southern leaders who had been appointed in Indian Territory.

He also protested against Confederate's prejudice against the Native American troops, arguing that his soldiers were not "paid as promptly nor equipped as thoroughly as other soldiers." He focused much of his wrath, though, on the encroaching Union army, especially what he referred to as a "mongrel force" of "hostile Indians, negroes and one battallion of Kansas troops," who had gained possession of Fort Gibson, a strategic

In this letter, written in September, 1862, Cherokee leader John Ross assured President Lincoln of his tribe's support for the Union. Lincoln, mindful of Ross's earlier pledge to the Confederacy, responded with caution and some skepticism.

Honey Springs Battlefield

1863 Honey Springs Battlefield
  Road
Checotah, OK 74426
918-473-5572
*http://checotah.lakewebs.net/
  honeysprings*

NRIS 7000848
NPS

DATE OF BATTLE
1863

SIGNIFICANCE
On July 17, 1863, Union and Confederate soldiers clashed in the biggest battle to occur in Indian Territory. Native Americans fought on both sides of the battle. The Union was victorious, securing control of the Indian Territory for the Federal government for the remainder of the war.

point that stood in the middle of the Indian Territory, specifically in Cherokee country.

Indeed, much of the military action in the Indian Territory focused on Fort Gibson, a military outpost near present-day Muskogee, Oklahoma, not far from the Arkansas border. Located at the confluence of the Arkansas, Grand, and Verdigris rivers, the fort was constructed in 1824. It remained an active post until the U.S. government turned it over to the Cherokee Nation in 1857.

When the Civil War began, Confederate forces occupied the fort, but they were driven off by Union troops in April 1863. From this point on, the Union army maintained a strong and active presence at Fort Gibson, which served to minimize the Confederate presence in the Indian Territory. In response to this Federal strength, Stand Watie devoted his efforts to dislodging the Union troops from the fort.

On July 1 and 2, 1863, he led Confederate cavalry units in a raid on a large supply train on the way to Fort Gibson from Kansas. The train was successfully defended, but the attack convinced Union leaders of the need for a preventive counterattack against Watie and the other Confederate forces, who had made their own encampment at Honey Springs Depot, twenty miles southwest of the fort.

Honey Springs Depot was a rural and wooded spot that straddled the Texas Road, a critical transportation route in the area situated along the Honey Springs stream. No settlements or villages marked the landscape, although there was one house and a few depot buildings used by the Confederates to store food and supplies. Never a permanent settlement, Honey Springs Depot provided an important watering and provision point for travelers on the Texas Road. In July 1863, it also provided a base for Confederate troops, who hoped to retake Fort Gibson.

Consequently, on July 16, 1863, Union Major General James Blunt led three thousand men, including members of the First and Second Indian Home Guard, out of Fort Gibson, across the Arkansas River, and toward the Confederate outpost where six thousand troops were waiting under the command of Brigadier General Douglas H. Cooper. The two forces converged on July 17, in a heavily wooded area a mile and a half from Honey Springs, along Elk Creek

The attack, known as the Battle of Honey Springs, was the largest and most significant of the eighty-nine Civil War engagements in the Indian Territory and signaled the end of any noteworthy Confederate resistance in the region. It also pitted a diverse force of white, black, and Indian Union soldiers against an enemy, which included some of the principle Native American regiments that had allied themselves with the Confederacy.

Although the Confederates brought superior numbers to the battle, and used the surrounding brush and timber to conceal themselves from the enemy, the battle proved to be a lopsided victory for the Union. The First Regiment Kansas Colored Volunteers, in particular, played a significant role in leading the charge against the Southern troops, having learned shortly before the battle of the Confederate government's decision to treat captured black soldiers with extreme severity.

The Confederates, meanwhile, suffered from poor equipment and ammunition. Despite their initial enthusiasm and determination, the Confederate Indian troops at Honey Springs soon became disheartened by the lack of dry gunpowder. According to General Cooper, "The Choctaws went at [the enemy], giving the war-whoop, and succeeded in checking the advance of the enemy until their force could be concentrated and all brought up." But, said Cooper, the Choctaws then became "discouraged on account of the worthless ammunition" and fell back to the rear of the line.

Overwhelmed by the Union force and their superior weaponry, the Confederates withdrew from the field and retreated from all their positions on Elk Creek. While retreating, the Confederates set fire to the Honey Springs Depot.

The Union troops managed to capture one of the commissary buildings, which contained large quantities of food, before it burned. They also seized three to four hundred sets of handcuffs housed in one of the depot buildings, which were meant for imprisoning captured African-American soldiers. Seventy-five Federals and 134 Confederates were either killed or wounded in that day's fighting, and forty-seven Confederate soldiers were imprisoned. The battle preserved Fort Gibson as a Union stronghold.

Stand Watie, who had now replaced John Ross as the Cherokee Nation's Principal Chief, left the Battle of

Honey Springs unscathed but more exasperated with the Confederates' inability to drive the Union enemy out of Indian Territory. Watie was determined to pursue his own campaign, if not to further the Confederate cause, then to further his own battle with his Cherokee opponents.

Indeed, in the summer and fall of 1864, Watie, now a Confederate brigadier general, led several successful raids against Union supply trains, and managed to seize hundreds of mules and horses while inflicting numerous casualties on the Union forces. But by this point, the main action of the war had shifted even further east in an all-out effort to stem the tide of Sherman's march. The Confederates had few resources or soldiers to spare for what now seemed like a lost cause in the region west of the Mississippi River. On June 23, 1865, Watie surrendered, one month after the Confederate commander of all troops west of the Mississippi River had already laid down his arms.

The end of the war brought little peace to the Cherokee Nation. The Cherokee National Council passed an act of amnesty for those who had fought on the side of the South; but Watie and many of his supporters

A Cherokee Letter to the Confederacy

Shortly after the Battle of Honey Springs, Cherokee leader Stand Watie wrote this letter to the Confederate governor in charge of the Creek nation, demanding more support from the Confederate government for the fight in Indian territory.

EXECUTIVE OFFICE, CHEROKEE NATION,
AUGUST 9, 1863.

HIS EXCELLENCY THE GOVERNOR
OF THE CREEK NATION:

Sir: The condition of affairs in the Indian country inclines me to address you upon the subject of paramount importance to Creeks as well as Cherokees, viz, the prospect of adequate assistance from the Confederate States against our enemies, and the ability of the Indians, unassisted, to maintain their rights and defend their homes. It is now more than a year since our foes invaded in force the Cherokee Nation. They have desolated the land and robbed the people, until scarcely a Southern family is left east and north of the Arkansas River. The friends of the South have almost as one man taken up arms in the Southern cause, and have, with their brothers of the other Nations, struck many blows upon their enemies. The promised protection of the Confederate Government, owing, I am compelled to say, to the glaring inefficiency of its subordinate agents, has accomplished nothing; it has been a useless and expensive pageant; an object for the success of our enemies and the shame of our friends. I fear we can reasonably look for no change for the better, but that the Indians will have at last to rely upon themselves alone in the defense of their country. I believe it is in the power of the Indians unassisted, but united and determined, to hold their country. We cannot expect to do this without serious losses and many trials and privations; but if we possess the spirit of our fathers, and are resolved never to be enslaved by an inferior race, and trodden under the feet of an ignorant and insolent foe, we, the Creeks, Choctaws, Chickasaws, Seminoles, and Cherokees, never can be conquered by the Kansas jayhawkers, renegade Indians, and runaway negroes. It requires at this time, and will as long as the war shall last, all the Yankee forces of Missouri to hold that State against the friends of the South within her limits. The multitude of soldiers that the North has now, or may yet bring into the field, will have abundant occupation elsewhere, so that the only expectation of the North to conquer the Indian Nation is in the traitors that have deserted us, the negroes they have stolen from us, and a few Kansas jayhawkers they can spare from that detestable region. Shall we suffer ourselves to be subjugated and enslaved by such a class? Never!

I have written to Lieut. Gen. E. Kirby Smith and the Commissioner of Indian Affairs upon these matters. I hope soon to know positively whether we are to receive effective assistance from the Confederate Government, or whether the Indians must defend themselves alone and unaided.

VERY RESPECTFULLY, YOUR OBEDIENT SERVANT,

STAND WATIE,

PRINCIPAL CHIEF OF THE CHEROKEES

received no pardon. Even more, the U.S. government decided to treat the Cherokees as a single group of Confederate allies, not as a divided tribe. Thus the tribe was forced to forego any exclusive rights it had to its land in Indian Territory.

As with other Indian communities, the Cherokees had also been economically and psychologically weakened by their wartime experiences. Also like the other American Indians in the postwar period, the Cherokees had no recognized legal standing in the United States. As the federal government pursued an expansionist and more aggressive policy against Native Americans in the postwar years, the Cherokees as well as the other tribes of the west, were often ill-prepared for the fight.

In the 1870s and 1880s, whether they had fought on the side of the Union or on the side of the Confederacy, the American Indian population found itself under relentless assault by the U.S. government. The leaders of that assault were often the very same men—such as Philip Sheridan and William Sherman—who had emerged as heroes of the Civil War and now gained new reputations as ruthless Indian fighters.

Today, the Honey Springs historic site greatly resembles the battlefield of 1863. The Honey Springs still flow and, as it was in the nineteenth century, the site remains mostly wooded and rural. The Texas Road, which originally divided the battle area, no longer exists. But the foundation of the old powder house still stands. The Honey Springs battlefield area is currently owned and maintained by the Oklahoma Historical Society.

ARMSTRONG ACADEMY SITE

Bokchito, OK 74726
*http://www.choctawnation.com
/history/choctaw_nation_
history.htm*
NHL

Armstrong Academy was an American Indian boarding school, run by missionaries, that taught farming, manual labor, and basic subjects to Native Americans. In 1849, fifty-five pupils lived at Armstrong. Ten years later, on the eve of the Civil War, more than nine hundred Choctaw students attended various schools, some of them at the Armstrong Academy. When the war began, Choctaws relocated their capital to this academy in order to remove it from the war zone. The building served as the Choctaw National Capitol from 1863 to 1883.

JOHN ROSS HOUSE

PO Box 863
Rossville, GA 30741
706-375-7702
*http://ngeorgia.com/site/
rosshouse.html*
NHL

Built in 1797, this two-story log house was the home of Cherokee Chief John Ross, prior to the Cherokee removal to Oklahoma. The house contains various Cherokee writings, furnishings, and pictures.

FORT GIBSON

907 N Garrison
Fort Gibson, OK 74434
918-478-4088
*http://www.ok-history.mus.ok.us
/gibson/gibson1.html*
NHL

During the war, the Union occupied Fort Davis, located near Fort Gibson. Then, in 1863, it reactivated Fort Gibson and occupied it to keep control of the Indian Territory. Confederate forces were stopped from occupying the fort after the Battle of Honey Springs. Some original buildings still remain.

PEA RIDGE NATIONAL MILITARY PARK

PO Box 700
Pea Ridge, AR 72751
501-451-8122
www.nps.gov/peri
NPS

On March 7 and 8, 1862, nearly twenty-six thousand soldiers fought at the battle of Pea Ridge to determine whether Missouri would remain under the control of Federal forces. Among the participants in the battle were eight hundred Cherokees who fought on the Confederate side and

managed to capture a battery of artillery. The historic site includes a newly renovated visitor center and two-and-a-half miles of the Trail of Tears. It remains one of the most well-preserved battlefields in the United States today.

TRAIL OF TEARS STATE PARK ARCHAEOLOGICAL SITE

Cape Girardeau County, MO 63701
573-334-6946
*http://rosecity.net/tears/
tears1.html*
NPS

Located along the Mississippi River in Cape Girardeau County, Missouri, this park commemorates the forced relocation of the Cherokee from their native homeland in the southeastern United States to the Indian Territory (present-day Oklahoma). In the winter of 1838–39, the Cherokee passed through the region in which the park is located. They made a treacherous crossing over the Mississippi River from Illinois to Missouri. The two-mile portion of the Trail of Tears route, which can be found in this park, is part of the National Park Service's Trail of Tears National Historic Trail. The visitor center provides information on the history of the forced relocation.

Andersonville National Historic Site

Andersonville, Ga.

A Prison Site of the Confederacy

In its two years of operation, Andersonville Prison housed about forty-five thousand Union inmates in an extremely overcrowded and unsanitary setting. Although the death rate was deplorable, it was exceeded by the Confederate prison at Salisbury, North Carolina where 34 percent of the 10,321 men died.

O nly sixteen years old when the Civil War began, Dorance Atwater had to receive his parents' permission to enlist in a Connecticut cavalry regiment. In 1863, three days after the battle of Gettysburg, Atwater was captured by Confederates while carrying military dispatches.

At first, the Connecticut soldier was imprisoned at Belle Isle, a Confederate jail near Richmond, Virginia, but then he was transferred to a newly opened prison at Andersonville, Georgia, in February 1864. Along with his comrades, Atwater spent his time at Andersonville Prison, living in makeshift tents and hovels, eating rotted food and drinking contaminated water, and suffering through debilitating diseases.

Unlike other prisoners however, Atwater received a special assignment. Because of his fine handwriting, he was ordered to keep an official account of Union prisoners' deaths for the Confederate surgeon at Andersonville Prison. Few tasks could have been more grim, for by the

fall of 1864, Atwater often counted more than one hundred dead on a single day. By the time of the war's conclusion, nearly thirteen thousand of the forty-five thousand Union prisoners at Andersonville had died in this notorious place of confinement, mostly from disease and starvation.

Faced with an increasing prison population, and anxious to move Union prisoners away from the main fields of war, the Confederate government had decided, at the end of 1863, to begin construction on a prison site in rural southwest Georgia. The region they chose was remote and sparsely populated, consisting of alternating fields and woodlands. Moreover, in the 1860s this part of Georgia possessed little agricultural significance, but it was relatively accessible to the railroad and the state's extensive pine forests. A good water supply flowed through the area's creeks and streams.

Ultimately, Confederate officials located a site in Sumter County, about fifty miles from the Alabama border, and laid the foundation for a prison that would be known officially as Camp Sumter. However, it became notorious under the name of the nearby village of Andersonville. Using pine logs, Southerners built a stockade around a sloping, open field of sixteen acres, planning for a prison population of ten thousand.

A hospital was located within the stockade at first, but then was moved outside the southeast corner. A morgue was situated outside the south gate of the stockade. But no barracks had been constructed when the first prisoners, including Dorance Atwater, began arriving in February 1864. Inmates used whatever was available to construct rude tents and shelters called "shebangs," based on the Irish word "shebeen," which referred to a low-class, unlicensed or illegal drinking establishment. A few shebangs were ready for occupancy by October 1864.

The prison population swelled from twenty-three thousand men held there in June 1864, to more than thirty-two thousand a few months later. Although the stockade had been expanded to enclose twenty-six acres, the Confederates were completely unable to offer adequate provisions for the men. Indeed, the chronic shortages, which the South faced toward the end of the war, made it hard for Southerners to feed themselves, let alone Union prisoners. They lacked the materials to

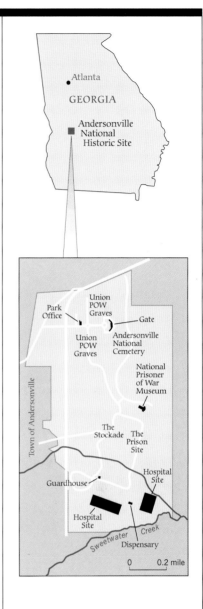

construct tents; they lacked boards and nails for erecting buildings; and they lacked the administrative awareness that might have allowed them to avoid the poor and often unsanitary conditions that plagued the Andersonville Prison from the outset.

A small stream running through the camp provided the prison population with its only source of water, and it soon became contaminated. A cookhouse and a bakery, located upstream from the stockade, dumped refuse into the prisoners' drinking water. The prisoners' latrines, situated right next to the stream, frequently overflowed into the creek when the rain was heavy. The water, explained one Vermont soldier, "isn't fit for a [h]og for it runs through the camp & every night & morning the cooks empty their greasy [water] & filth in the [b]rook & the stench that arises from the watter is enough to suffocate [any] [common] man god help us."

Like drinkable water, decent food was also nearly nonexistent. Facing extreme food shortages for their own soldiers, the Confederacy provided Andersonville prisoners with the most meager—and usually rotten— food supplies: small bits of raw cornmeal mixed with swamp water or soup containing pea pods and dirt.

Andersonville prison, shown here in a birdseye view from the southeast, first began accepting Union prisoners in the beginning of 1864 to accommodate prisoners being held at Belle Isle near Richmond. Confederates preferred this Georgia site as it could not be as easily disrupted by Union troops.

Under such desperate circumstances, some inmates tried to escape by digging tunnels under the stockade wall. Nearly all were recaptured. Others, having lost all hope of survival, chose to cross the "dead line," the no-man's land between the prisoners' enclosure and the stockade wall. Once spotted beyond the dead line, a prisoner was shot without question.

Had the North and the South maintained a system of regular prisoner exchanges through the latter part of the war, Dorance Atwater and his comrades might have been released from the miserable conditions of Andersonville. Early in the war, prisoners had been regularly and routinely exchanged, making confinement for inmates on both sides relatively brief. In addition, both sides at first relied chiefly on makeshift accommodations in civilian jails, sections of training camps, and walled-in areas of forts for housing prisoners and only later established more official prison camps. These camps, like the one at Andersonville, became more and more necessary in 1863 when the prisoner exchange broke down.

The official Confederate policy failed to recognize captured black soldiers as legitimate prisoners of war and therefore refused to make them eligible for the prisoner exchanges that occurred during 1861 and 1862. Instead, the Confederate Congress declared its intention to execute or enslave captured black soldiers and, certainly on a number of occasions, the Confederate army carried out the threat.

The Lincoln administration, then committed to a program of emancipation and to the enlistment of African-American soldiers, declined to cooperate with the exchange of prisoners until the Confederate policy changed. As a result, the number of prisoners in both the Northern and the Southern confinements began to mount, and the conditions in prisons throughout the country began to deteriorate. Indeed, a number of Northern prisons forced many Confederate inmates to endure cramped and unsanitary conditions, as well as extreme food shortages.

In May 1864, Secretary of War Edwin Stanton ordered that rations be reduced for Confederate prisoners and other severe measures be introduced. All told, about 215,000 Confederates were held in Union prisons, with 26,000, about 12 percent, perishing while in captivity..

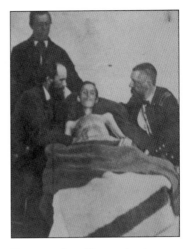

Pictures such as this one, showing a horribly emaciated Union soldier upon his release from a Southern prison, greatly aroused Northern anger against Confederates and their seemingly inhumane prison policy. "Retaliation," wrote the New York Times, "is a terrible thing, but the miseries and pains and the slowly wasting life of our brethren and friends in those horrible prisons is a worse thing."

Andersonville National Historic Site

Route 1, Box 800
Andersonville, GA 31711
912-924-0343
www.nps.gov/ande

NRIS 70000070
NHL/NPS

DATE BUILT
1863–64

BUILDER
Confederate troops

SIGNIFICANCE
Andersonville held roughly forty-five thousand Union prisoners between February 14, 1864, and the end of April, 1865. Of those, thirteen thousand died in the camp. Andersonville National Historic Site serves as a memorial to American prisoners in all wars. The 495-acre park consists of the historic prison site and the national cemetery. The National Prisoner of War Museum opened at Andersonville in 1988.

Conditions in Confederate prisons were, on the whole, deadlier and more difficult, largely due to chronic food shortages and the problem of maintaining prisoners in a land ravaged by war. Of the 144,000 Union men confined in Confederate prisons, about 30,000, almost 21 percent, did not survive. And no Confederate prison had more lethal or deplorable conditions than Andersonville.

One of the most brutalizing aspects of Andersonville Prison life was the degree to which the camp's inmates abused and tormented one another. Gangs of prisoners frequently preyed upon weaker inmates, stealing food from many and even killing some. William "Mosby" Collins led the most notorious of these gangs and embarked on a campaign of terror during the spring and summer of 1864. With Mosby encountering little restraint from Confederate guards, Andersonville Prison's commander eventually agreed to allow the inmates to try Mosby's gang for their crimes. In July 1864, a jury of Andersonville prisoners passed sentence on Mosby and his conspirators. Their executions followed swiftly.

Outside the prison walls, Andersonville Prison was becoming known, in the North and the South, for its atrocious conditions. A Georgia professor of medicine visited the site and found the conditions for hospital patients to be especially deplorable. Many of them, he remarked, were "literally incrusted with dirt and filth and covered with vermin." Local Georgia residents decried the horrible conditions of the place and its inhabitants; some even tried to bring fresh produce to the starving prisoners.

In the North, Andersonville Prison came to stand as a symbol for the worst abuses and atrocities of Jefferson Davis's government. Some saw the death rate at Andersonville as an indication of an intentional Confederate policy to deplete the ranks of the Union army. When several Andersonville Prison escapees arrived at General William T. Sherman's camp on Thanksgiving Day 1864, their emaciated and ragged condition encouraged Sherman's men to renew their course of punishment against the Confederacy.

By this point, with Sherman's march bringing the war into the heart of the Georgia countryside, many Andersonville prisoners had been moved to other prisons along the Georgia and South Carolina coasts. In April

Outraged at the horrendous suffering endured by Union soldiers at Andersonville, Northerners vented their rage against the Confederate prison's commander, Henrich Wirz. Wirz became the only Confederate to be executed by the federal government in the aftermath of the war.

1865, the last of the Andersonville prisoners was sent to a camp near Vicksburg, Mississippi. Many lost their lives when an explosion rocked the transport ship that carried them along the Mississippi River. Those who survived this tragic accident were soon released. The next month, Union forces occupied the Andersonville site and arrested Captain Henrich Wirz, the Swiss-born commander of the prison's interior. Northerners now began to see firsthand some of the atrocious conditions at the site, especially as the images and stories of Andersonville survivors became known.

With outrage mounting in the North over the Andersonville Prison atrocities, many focused their anger on Wirz, holding him responsible for the thousands of deaths among the prisoners. Although there was no evidence of Wirz's personal responsibility in the deaths of prisoners, the commander and his prison became symbolic of what Northerners saw as Confederate barbarism, especially in the months after Abraham Lincoln's assassination. Tried and sentenced by a military tribunal, Wirz became the only Confederate to be executed by the federal government in the aftermath of the war.

For his part, Dorance Atwater also wanted to focus the nation's attention on Andersonville, although with a somewhat different purpose in mind. Learning that the renowned Union nurse Clara Barton was anxious to begin the process of identifying thousands of missing Union soldiers, Atwater wrote to Barton and told her of the records he had kept of the Andersonville dead. Barton realized that this extensive documentation could

Nearly thirteen thousand men perished at Andersonville prison. Most of the dead were identified, and their gravesites marked, as a result of the meticulous records kept by Union prisoner Dorance Atwater.

provide answers for many suffering Union families, who had yet to learn the fate of their loved ones. Although Atwater's records would sadly confirm the death of thousands of soldiers, they would also provide needed information to Union families, who wished to know those soldiers' final resting places.

In July 1865, Dorance Atwater returned to the place of his wartime confinement, now accompanied by Barton and several government officials. Using Atwater's records, they identified and marked the graves of close to thirteen thousand Union soldiers, who had died at the prison camp. In this way, their actions made Andersonville more than just a site associated with Confederate brutality in Northern minds; it was now also a place to honor the deceased Union prisoners of war.

For her pioneering role in this mission, Clara Barton came to occupy an even more revered place in the hearts of many Americans. She had tended to the sick and suffering soldiers during the long years of war; in the war's aftermath, her work at Andersonville brought at least some sense of peace to thousands of families throughout the North.

Barton also believed that Andersonville should be preserved as a site of national historical significance, as a special place for remembering the sacrifices and suffering of Union soldiers. "It seems fitting," she explained in

Some of the higher-ranking members of the Confederate armed forces, including these men from the upper ranks of the Confederate Navy, were imprisoned in Fort Warren in Boston Harbor.

Fort Warren: A Union Prison in Boston Harbor

Fort Warren, located on George's Island in Boston Harbor, was one of the most important prison sites used by the Union administration for Confederate inmates. Although it never held great numbers of prisoners, the fort confined noted Confederate officers and political leaders as well as civilian sympathizers.

During the war, the fort held hundreds of political prisoners, many of whom were targeted by the Lincoln administration in an attempt to silence possible Confederate sympathizers, especially in the border states. Hundreds of Confederate soldiers, and some of their commanding officers, also endured confinement at Fort Warren. But the prison experience for elite officers and civilians could vary dramatically from that of the common Confederate soldiers.

Many of the fort's wealthier civilian and officer inmates could secure meals from local merchants and enjoy gifts of food and other luxuries from friends in the North and the South. One Maryland inmate described his fare at Fort Warren as "equal to any of the hotels; the only trouble is I eat too much for so little exercise." However, Confederate soldiers who lacked money and connections, had to make do with much simpler and more limited rations.

Perhaps the most luxurious meals were enjoyed by James Mason and John Slidell, who arrived in Fort Warren in November 1861. As Confederate commissioners to Great Britain and France, the two diplomats had set sail for Europe to convince British and French leaders to lend their support to the new Southern nation. Viewing their mission as a violation of the Union blockade, Captain Charles Wilkes intercepted their ship and imprisoned them at Fort Warren. Having important connections to wealthy Northerners, Mason and Slidell ate well during their brief stay at Fort Warren.

Their arrest, however, triggered a diplomatic crisis for the Lincoln administration, when the British government expressed outrage at the diplomats' "impressment" and raised the specter of a larger European conflict for the Union. By New Year's, Mason and Slidell were released and the crisis with England had been averted.

The relatively relaxed conditions that prisoners experienced at Fort Warren in 1861 and 1862 came to an end in the later years of the war. Prisoners' hopes for exchange diminished as negotiations collapsed between the North and the South. The Union administration began to impose harsher treatment on inmates at Fort Warren and other Northern prisons. They limited the flow of gifts to the prisoners. They more often demanded the close confinement of Confederate inmates, and had greater numbers of prisoners shackled in irons.

At the very end of the war, Fort Warren received its final contingent of Civil War prisoners: several members of Robert E. Lee's staff and Confederate Vice President Alexander Stephens, who was captured when the Davis administration fled Richmond. By October 1865, as prisoners throughout the North won release, Fort Warren ceased to function as a Civil War prison.

In the second part of the nineteenth century, Fort Warren received a number of noteworthy modifications, including the installation of more modern guns and gun mounts. In 1958 the fort came under the oversight of the Metropolitan District Commission of the Commonwealth of Massachusetts, which maintains it as a national historic landmark.

FORT WARREN

Georges Island
Boston, MA
617-223-8666
www.bostonislands.org/georges/
  html
NHL

This fort, located on Georges Island, is part of the Boston Harbor Islands National Park Area. It was built to protect Boston Harbor, was constructed with outer walls of Quincy granite that are eight feet thick. Fort Warren was a prison for Confederate leaders and officers, including Alexander Stephens, vice president of the Confederate States of America.

an official report she prepared on Andersonville Prison, "that it should be preserved as one of the sanctuaries of the nation, and be in due time decorated with appropriate honors."

To some extent, Barton's hope for Andersonville Prison has been realized, although for many it remains a controversial place. In 1891, a Union veterans' group in Georgia purchased the Andersonville Prison site with the purpose of creating a memorial park.

In 1911, the land of both the former prison site and the cemetery was donated to the U.S. government, eventually coming under the jurisdiction of the National Park Service. Over the years, various monuments have been constructed, paying tribute to the soldiers of various Northern states who died at the prison. Monuments have also been constructed in honor of Clara Barton and the women's auxiliary group that oversaw the park site for a number of years. Today, the Andersonville site is meant to serve as a memorial, not just to the Union men who died there, but to all American prisoners of war in all conflicts.

A few people, however, have tried to tell a different story. Outside the park area in the town of Andersonville, a Confederate women's memorial group erected a statue to Captain Wirz, proclaiming him a scapegoat of Northern postwar anger. Some white Southerners continue to resent the preoccupation with Andersonville Prison and its position as a national historic site, believing that conditions there were generally no worse than conditions in other Civil War prisons.

Most historians, however, believe that Andersonville represented the worst aspects of the Civil War prison experience. They do not hold individual Confederates personally responsible nor believe the Confederate government practiced an intentional policy of brutality aimed at reducing the ranks of the Union army. Rather, most believe that many of the horrors at Andersonville Prison resulted from the shortages and desperate circumstances that plagued the Confederacy toward the end of the war. Some suggest that the horribly overcrowded conditions came as an unintended consequence of the decision to end the prisoner exchange program that was suspended after the Confederates refused to treat both black and white prisoners equally.

Appomattox Court House National Historical Park

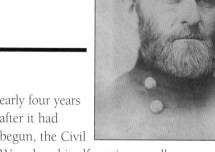

Appomattox, Va.

A Place of Surrender

In 1865, Ulysses Grant (above) and Robert E. Lee negotiated the surrender of Lee's army at Wilmer McLean's home (below) in Appomattox Court House, Virginia. This signaled the near conclusion of the Civil War. General Ulysses Grant was hailed as a hero in the North at the end of the Civil War. His wartime popularity spurred on his nomination by the Republican Party for whom he became the presidential standard-bearer in 1868 and 1872.

Nearly four years after it had begun, the Civil War played itself out in a small, remote town in central Virginia, ninety miles east of Richmond. At last recognizing the futility, if not the impossibility, of further military action, Confederate commander Robert E. Lee agreed to meet Union leader Ulysses S. Grant in the town, known as Appomattox Court House, on April 9, 1865.

Here, in the home of one of the town's citizens, the two Civil War generals agreed to the terms of surrender for Robert E. Lee's Army of Northern Virginia. Although scattered fighting continued after Lee's submission, Appomattox Court House came to symbolize, in the days and years that followed, the final moment of the Civil War and the beginning of the nation's reunification.

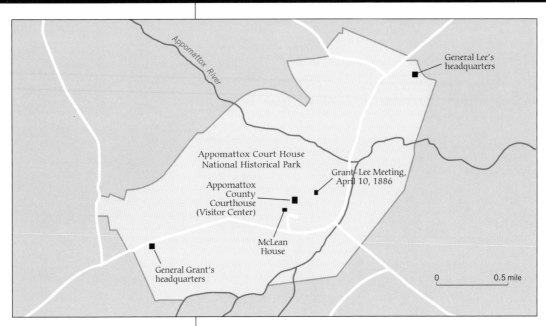

In the early years of the nineteenth century, the town of Clover Hill, named for the local tavern, was little more than a stagecoach stop on the way from Richmond to Lynchburg. In 1845, when the town became the seat for the new county of Appomattox, it was renamed Appomattox Court House, following a Virginia custom of using the county name, followed by "court house," to designate these administrative seats.

Situated on a small incline in a region of gently rolling hills overlooking the Appomattox River, the town stood in one of Virginia's prime tobacco-growing regions. Many of the citizens of Appomattox Court House, in fact, made their living from the tobacco trade, with the bulk of the labor performed by slaves.

By the summer of 1861, the people of Appomattox Court House, like their neighbors throughout the South, had become engulfed in the Civil War crisis. Men had departed for distant battlefields, while those at home made monetary and material contributions to help the war effort. At least one family had gradually sought out the town of Appomattox Court House as a refuge from the tumult of war. Wilmer McLean, a farmer in Prince William County, Virginia, owned an expansive piece of property overlooking Bull Run Creek near Manassas.

When Union and Confederate troops converged toward Bull Run for the first major military engagement of the war, Wilmer McLean found his home transformed into a Confederate military headquarters. When the battle ended, McLean's house contained dozens of wounded and dying Southerners, who received their medical care in this makeshift hospital.

One year later, when fighting returned to the Bull Run area, Wilmer McLean decided that he would rather not have the Civil War waged in his backyard. Life in a more remote Virginia spot, he felt, would be considerably safer for his family and his then-pregnant wife. Using the rent money he had collected from the Confederate government for the use of his Bull Run property, McLean bought two taverns and several surrounding lots in Appomattox Court House. In 1862, Wilmer McLean moved from the war's first bloody fields to Appomatox Court House in the relatively tranquil backcountry of Virginia's Piedmont district.

Three years later, in the spring of 1865, the war again found the McLean family, even here in their rural Virginia refuge. Once more, troops converged on the McLeans, but now those troops were no longer new recruits; they were worn and weary veterans moving into the war's final hours. The movement toward Appomattox Court House

Robert E. Lee moved his men toward the town of Appomattox Court House in April 1865, hoping to find some much-needed supplies for his suffering soldiers. Outnumbering Lee by about five or six to one, Grant was able to compel Lee's surrender in this small Virginia town.

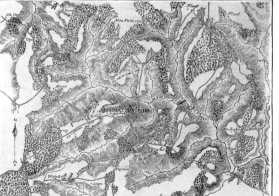

MAP OF APPOMATTOX COURT HOUSE AND VICINITY.

Showing the relative positions of the Confederate and Federal Armies at the time of General R. E. Lee's Surrender, April 9th, 1865.

Lee's Head-Quarters.

Grant's Head-Quarters.

McLean's House.

Appomattox Court House.

GEN. LEE'S FAREWELL TO HIS ARMY.

Place where Six Arms were Stacked.

Appomattox Court House National Historical Park

Highway 24
P. O. Box 218
Appomattox, VA 24522
804-352-8987
www.nps.gov/apco

NRIS 66000827
NPS

DATE BUILT
1848 (McLean house); reconstructed in 1950

ARCHITECT
Charles Raine

SIGNIFICANCE
Robert E. Lee surrendered his
Army of Northern Virginia to
Union General Ulysses S. Grant
here on April 9, 1865. The site
includes twenty-seven nineteenth-century buildings and the
village of Appomattox Court
House. Some buildings, including the McLean home, where the
actual surrender was negotiated,
were reconstructed in the twentieth century.

represented the final stage of Robert E. Lee's withdrawal
from his long-held outpost in Petersburg, Virginia.

Having shifted to a defensive war strategy in 1864,
in order to conserve his own resources and to force the
Union into risking greater casualties, Lee's army had
been entrenched around Petersburg since the late spring
of 1864. But as Federal troops began to close in on both
Richmond and Petersburg, Lee was forced to abandon
his position on April 2, 1865.

On that same day, Jefferson Davis, his family, and
his Confederate government fled Richmond, leaving the
Southern capital in the hands of the Union army.
Although the Union now controlled the seat of the
Confederacy, the war would not officially end as long as
there were combatants in the field ready and willing to
defend the Confederate cause.

With the hope of eventually joining forces with
Confederate General Joseph Johnston's men in North
Carolina, Robert E. Lee led his troops into Virginia's
southwest corner. However, by then starvation had taken
as much of a toll on Lee's soldiers as the pursuing Union
army. The Confederates continued moving west, mainly
in search of supplies. Aware of Lee's increasingly desperate circumstances, Union commander Ulysses Grant
looked for an opening to force Lee's surrender.

The opportunity seemed at hand when Grant
learned that Union General William Sheridan had positioned his troops at Appomattox Station, the railroad
depot near Appomattox Court House, with the intention
of capturing several Confederate supply trains. On April 7,
Grant wrote to Lee and asked him to surrender. On
April 9, General John Gordon made a final attempt to
pierce the Union line that stood between his hungry
Confederates and the supply depot. When Gordon's
attempt failed, Lee agreed that the time had come to discuss an end to the hostilities.

With vast numbers of Southern soldiers deserting
the army, Lee saw little chance for a battlefield victory
against the encroaching Federals. The prospect of sending
his troops home to keep up the fight by other means
seemed an equally unappealing alternative. By midday on
April 9, Grant had received Lee's request for a meeting
to discuss a surrender, and by two o'clock that same
afternoon, Grant was on his way to meet his
Confederate counterpart.

Prior to Grant's arrival, one of Lee's aides had ridden ahead toward the courthouse building in Appomattox to secure a suitable location where the generals could convene. By chance, he encountered one of Appomattox's recent refugees, Wilmer McLean. When asked for his advice about a gathering place, McLean at first recommended an old and somewhat dilapidated building in the town. When that suggestion was deemed unsuitable, McLean offered his own home, which stood on a lot west of the courthouse building. A former tavern, McLean's house was a large and comfortable two-story brick structure with a chimney on each of the side walls. McLean ushered Lee and his staff officers into the first-floor parlor, where they sat and waited for Grant.

After a brief discussion of their old army experiences in Mexico, Lee and Grant discussed surrender. Grant's terms were simple and straightforward: soldiers and officers would be paroled after surrendering their arms; weapons and supplies would become captured property; and soldiers, as long as they maintained their parole, were free to return home.

Upon further discussion with Lee, Grant also agreed that those Confederates who owned their own horses—which was true for most—could take them home. The

The surrender of Robert E. Lee to Ulysses S. Grant, in the parlor of Wilmer McLean's home in Appomattox Court House, became one of the most hallowed moments of the Civil War.

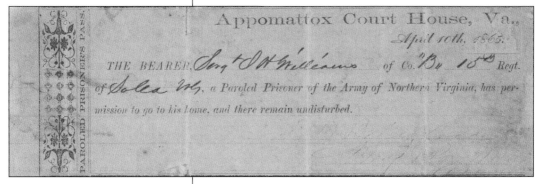

PAROLED PRISONER'S PASS.

Appomattox Court House, Va.,
April 10th, 1865.

THE BEARER *Serg't J H Williams* of Co. *"B"* *15th* Regt.
of *So Ca Vol*, a Paroled Prisoner of the Army of Northern Virginia, has permission to go to his home, and there remain undisturbed.

As part of Ulysses Grant's generous surrender terms to Lee's troops, Confederate soldiers were issued passes that granted them parole and allowed them to return to their homes in the South.

Union commander also agreed to provide rations from the captured supply trains to the nearly starved troops. The terms did not extend to all Confederate soldiers, but only to those under Lee's command, about twenty-eight thousand men all told.

With the surrender meeting concluded, the McLean home instantly became a historic icon. Officers, who were present cleaned out the parlor, buying or taking many of the room's furnishings as souvenirs. When the scavenging had ended, the McLean parlor was a wreck. Despite his protests, Wilmer McLean's home had once again become a casualty of the Civil War.

In the end, more than just papers had to be signed and exchanged before the surrender could be formalized. Federal officers called for an official parade in which Confederate troops would pass before the Union army, and in a symbolic show of submission, place their surrendered weapons in a stack before the victors. On April 12, Confederate General Gordon led the defeated Southerners in a march between two lines of Federal troops. The march spread for more than a quarter-mile through the town of Appomattox Court House. Union troops, at the order of Union commander and Gettysburg hero Joshua Chamberlain, displayed a carry-arms salute as the Southerners passed.

In the multilayered legends that would be constructed in the postwar years, Chamberlain's salute to the vanquished foes would be seen as an opening gesture of brotherly reconciliation between enemies. In fact, it might not have been intended as anything more than a way to keep silence among the troops.

Much was made, too, of Grant's generous peace terms and of his subsequent order that the Union troops curtail excessive jubilation at the Confederates' capitulation. Thus, according to the postwar myths, the Appomattox

Lee Surrenders at Appomattox

 On April 9, 1865, while sitting in Wilmer McLean's house in Appomattox Court House, Confederate General Robert E. Lee and Union General Ulysses Grant signed this treaty, agreeing to the terms under which Lee's army would surrender.

Agreement entered into this day in regard to the surrender of the Army of Northern Virginia to the United States authorities.

1st. The troops shall march by brigades and detachments to a designated point, stack their arms, deposit their flags, sabers, pistols, &c., and from thence march to their homes under charge of their officers, superintended by their respective division and corps commanders, officers retaining their side arms, and the authorized number of private horses.

2nd. All public horses and public property of all kinds to be turned over to staff officers designated by the United States authorities.

3rd. Such transportation as may be agreed upon as necessary for the transportation of the private baggage of officers will be allowed to accompany the officers, to be turned over at the end of the trip to the nearest U.S. quartermasters, receipts being taken for the same.

4th. Couriers and mounted men of the artillery and cavalry, whose horses are their own private property, will be allowed to retain them.

5th. The surrender of the Army of Northern Virginia shall be construed to include all the forces operating with that army on the 8th instant, the date of commencement of negotiation for surrender, except such bodies of cavalry as actually made their escape previous to the surrender, and except also such pieces of artillery as were more than twenty miles from Appomattox Court-House at the time of surrender on the 9th instant.

JOHN GIBBON,
MAJOR-GENERAL OF VOLUNTEERS.

CHAS. GRIFFIN,
BREVET MAJOR-GENERAL, U.S. VOLUNTEERS.

W. MERRITT,
BREVET MAJOR-GENERAL.

J. LONGSTREET,
LIEUTENANT-GENERAL.

J. B. GORDON,
MAJOR-GENERAL.

W. N. PENDLETON,
BRIGADIER-GENERAL AND CHIEF OF ARTILLERY.

General Order No. 9

Head Quarters A. N. Va.
April 10th, 1865

After four years of arduous service marked by unsurpassed courage and fortitude the Army of Northern Virginia has been compelled to yield to overwhelming numbers & resources.

I need not tell the brave survivors of so many hard fought battles who have remained steadfast to the last that I have consented to the result from no distrust of them.

But feeling that valor and devotion could accomplish nothing that would compensate for the loss that must have attended the continuance of the contest I determined to avoid the useless sacrifice of those whose past services have endeared them to their countrymen.

By the terms of the agreement Officers and men can return to their homes and remain until exchanged. You will take with you the satisfaction that proceeds from the consciousness of duty faithfully performed, and I earnestly pray that a merciful God will extend to you his blessing and protection.

With an unceasing admiration of your constancy and devotion to your country and a grateful remembrance of your kind and generous consideration for myself I bid you an affectionate farewell.

R E Lee
Genl

Although some Confederate officials urged that Lee and his men refuse to surrender and, instead, undertake a prolonged guerilla conflict against the Union, Lee believed that an honorable surrender was the best course of action. In his General Order No. 9, Lee dispersed, and bade farewell, to the soldiers who had fought with him in the Army of Northern Virginia.

surrender, symbolized in both the meeting between Lee and Grant and the April 12 parade, set the tone for a national reunification.

As with all myths, this one contained elements of truth, but no doubt exaggerated their significance. Certainly some degree of sympathy and mutual respect was expressed by both Grant and Chamberlain in their encounters with the enemy. But a considerable amount of rancor and hostility persisted on both sides, as well as numerous political differences regarding the status of Southern whites and blacks in the postwar period. These differences left a gulf between the North and the South that could not be bridged simply with the gestures and rituals of the surrender at Appomattox Court House.

In many ways, it was the legends, more than the simple truths, that made Appomattox Court House a symbolic landmark of the American Civil War.

Numerous travelers made pilgrimages to visit the sites—especially the McLean house—where the surrender occurred. Yet, within five years of the war's conclusion, the house no longer belonged to Wilmer McLean.

Because of his failure to repay a loan, McLean had been forced to sell the house at a public auction in 1869. In 1891, it was resold to Myron Dunlap of Niagara Falls, New York, who hoped to capitalize on the home's legendary status by dismantling it and moving it to Chicago for display at the 1893 World's Fair. Unfortunately, the only part of Dunlap's plan to be realized was the dismantling. Until the 1940s, the former McLean home sat in its dismembered state, victim to vandals and decay.

When the U.S. Congress created the Appomattox Court House National Historical Monument in 1940, their plans called for a reconstruction of the house, a project at last completed in 1949. Today, the National Park Service maintains an 1,800-acre site that includes twenty-seven original nineteenth-century structures, among them the original Clover Hill Tavern built in 1819. The reconstructed McLean House, including a kitchen, ice house, and slave quarters, is also a part of this site.

RELATED SITES

BENNETT PLACE STATE HISTORIC SITE

4409 Bennett Memorial Road
Durham, NC 27705
919-383-4345
http://dcvb.durham.nc.us/group/ features/bennett_place.html
NHL/NPS

Confederate General Joseph E. Johnston surrendered to Union General William T. Sherman at Bennett Place on April 26, 1865, just seventeen days after Lee's surrender at Appomattox Court House. Johnston surrendered the largest number of troops during the Civil War. The site has a reconstructed farmhouse with outbuildings.

ULYSSES S. GRANT NATIONAL HISTORIC SITE

7400 Grant Road
St. Louis, MO 63123
314-842-3298
www.nps.org/ulsg
NPS

After the surrender at Appomattox Court House and the close of the Civil War, Ulysses S. Grant planned to retire to this Missouri home, known as White Haven, that he had shared with his wife Julia Dent Grant prior to the war. The 9.65-acre site, which consists of five historic structures, commemorates Grant's life and career in the military and as President of the United States.

Arlington House, The Robert E. Lee Memorial

McLean, Va.

A Final Resting Place for the Civil War Dead

Soon after the Civil War began, the Lee family estate at Arlington (below) came under Union occupation, serving as a huge military outpost that offered protection for the nation's capital. His outstanding military leadership made Robert E. Lee (above) a legend during and after the Civil War and transformed the sites associated with his life, such as Arlington House, into Civil War icons.

B y the 1830s, Robert E. Lee had made Arlington House his home. The property—which included a mansion, outbuildings, and an 1,100-acre estate in Arlington, Virginia—technically belonged to Lee's father-in-law, George Washington Parke Custis. But when Lee was not on one of his frequent army engineering assignments, he generally returned to Arlington, where his wife, Mary Custis Lee, continued to reside with her parents.

In 1857, with her father's death, the Arlington estate passed into Mary Lee's hands. Her ownership proved brief and tumultuous. In April 1861, Mary Lee and her children bade farewell to the Arlington estate as Federal troops moved south from Washington into the Confederacy. Neither Robert, Mary Lee, nor any of their children, would

ever again call this Virginia plantation their home. Instead, the land that once displayed the formal gardens of the Lee estate and was once tilled by the slaves of the Lee family would become a final resting place for the dead bodies of Civil War soldiers.

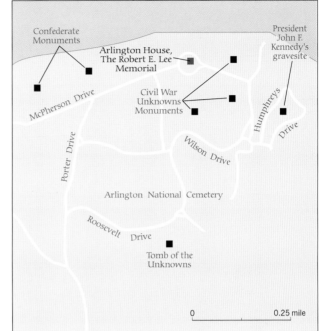

In 1778, John Parke Custis, son of Martha Washington, purchased an estate he called "Arlington" from the Alexander family. When John Custis's son, George, assumed ownership of the estate at the close of the American Revolution, he made plans to develop and embellish the property. Securing the assistance of George Hadfield, superintendent of construction of the U.S. Capitol building, George Custis oversaw the construction of a two-story Greek Revival mansion that would be known as Arlington House.

The work was completed, at least in part, by the Custis family slaves. Built of brick, with a stuccoed exterior, the building consists of a central two-story section flanked on either side by a one-story wing. The structure's most impressive features are the eight marbelized brick columns that sit on the large central portico. It was one of the first American buildings to incorporate the styles of Greek antiquity, making a visual connection between the Republican mission of the United States and the early Republican practices of ancient Greece.

Appropriately, the house sits on a hill overlooking Washington, D.C., just across the Potomac River, displaying its architectural tribute to the new government's Republican ideals. During George Custis's residence at Arlington, visitors could also make a visual connection to the nation's founding principles inside the house, thanks to the owner's collection of memorabilia associated with his adoptive father—and his grandmother's husband—George Washington.

When it was completed in 1818, Arlington House was a prime example of a Southern planter's residence. It revealed the power and wealth of a prominent Southern man, who could enjoy the leisure opportunities afforded by his home and estate, while he oversaw the labors of

Arlington House, The Robert E. Lee Memorial

George Washington Memorial Parkway
Turkey Run Park
McLean, VA 22101
703-235-1530
www.arlingtoncemetery.org
www.nps.gov/arho

NRIS 66000040
NPS

DATE BUILT
Arlington House, 1803;
cemetery established in 1864

ARCHITECT
George Hadfield

SIGNIFICANCE
The grounds and the house were once part of Robert E. Lee's plantation, until the property was taken over by the U.S. government during the Civil War to be used as an army camp and later as a Union cemetery. Restoration of the house began in 1925 under the auspices of the War Department. In 1955, it became a memorial to Robert E. Lee.

an expansive workforce of slaves he owned. The simply constructed outbuildings, lying to the west of the main house, provided rudimentary living quarters for the ninety or so slaves, who resided on the Arlington property.

Although Arlington House was a plantation, Custis never developed the full commercial potential of his land, and used the property mainly to sustain the estate's white and black inhabitants. Slaves at Arlington House cooked and served meals, cared for the gardens and grounds, managed the livestock, and kept the mansion clean and presentable.

The slaves were no doubt pressed into a frenzy of cleaning in the weeks leading up to June 30, 1831. On that day, Mary Custis married the young Lieutenant Robert E. Lee in the family parlor of Arlington House. When his army service allowed, Lee would return to Arlington to spend time with his in-laws, his wife, and his own growing family. Over the years, the Lees witnessed the birth of six of their seven children in this ancestral home.

Then, in 1857, with George Custis's death, Mary Lee became Arlington's new owner, although her ownership of the plantation's slaves was meant to be brief. According to the terms of the will, the Custis slaves at Arlington and at the other Custis properties were required to be freed by the year 1862. As the principal executor of George Custis's estate, Robert E. Lee assumed primary responsibility for the slaves' emancipation.

For their part, the bondsmen and women, who were fully aware of the terms of Custis' will, showed no inclination to let Lee backtrack on Custis's pledge. Various slaves, Lee complained in an 1858 letter to his son, have "rebelled against my authority—refused to obey my orders, & said they were as free as I was. . . . I succeeded in capturing them, however, tied them & lodged them in jail." Whatever Lee ultimately intended, in 1861 he found his attentions diverted from the problems of plantation management and slave liberation. With the outbreak of war, the slaves at Arlington House found their hopes of freedom temporarily dashed.

After the secession of Virginia in April 1861, Robert E. Lee resigned his commission in the U.S. Army and, soon after, accepted his new post with the Confederate military. Given the close proximity to Washington, D.C., life in Arlington House became increasingly

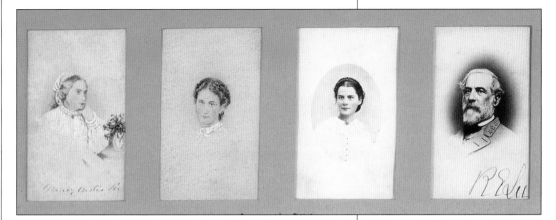

With his wife, Mary Custis Lee (far left), Robert E. Lee (far right) had several children, including daughters Mildred and Agnes (center). Of all of the Lee family members, Mary Custis Lee probably felt the loss of the Arlington home, her former ancestral estate, most keenly.

uncomfortable for Confederate sympathizers, and eventually untenable when Union troops moved into Virginia.

By May, Mary Lee and her children had left to take up residence at other family properties, not long before Arlington House fell into Federal hands. Distraught at this military occupation, Mary Lee wrote to General Irvin McDowell, the officer in charge, demanding consideration for herself and her possessions. "It never occurred to me," she wrote, "that I could be forced to sue for permission to enter my own home." She asked McDowell to send her some of her slaves still in bondage, and some of her personal belongings, a request that McDowell granted.

Ultimately, however, Mary Lee's distress over the fate of Arlington House could not be so easily redressed. Indeed, within a few months of the initial Federal occupation, the Arlington estate resembled an armed camp, serving as a critical Union defense post for the protection of the national capital. The possibility that the Lees might return to their northern Virginia plantation now seemed more and more remote. "As to our old home," Lee wrote to his wife at the end of 1861,

> if not destroyed, it will be difficult ever to be recognized. Even if the enemy had wished to preserve it, it would almost have been impossible. With the number of troops encamped around it, the change of officers, etc. the want of fuel, shelter, etc. & the dire necessities of war, it is vain to think of its being in a habitable condition.

As Lee predicted, the house had certainly become unsuitable for the family's habitation, having been transformed into military headquarters for the local commanding officers. Eventually, too, many of the family's possessions, including some of the Washington heirlooms, were removed from the house and taken to the Patent Office in Washington, D.C.

In 1864, when the U.S. government refused to allow Mary Lee to cross Union lines to pay the taxes on the estate, the property was quickly put up for auction and sold to the government for $26,800. At the urging of U.S. Quartermaster General Montgomery Meigs, two hundred acres of the Confederate commander's plantation were set aside for the creation of a national cemetery for those who had perished in the Union cause. With the death rate around Washington reaching staggering heights, burials commenced at the Arlington estate, even before the property had been legally acquired by the federal government.

By the time the war ended in the spring of 1865, more than 620,000 soldiers had died. Of these, about 360,000 had perished on the Union side; 260,000 for the Confederates. The Civil War produced the same number of American deaths as the combined total for all other wars Americans participated in through the Vietnam War. Many of the Civil War dead were buried in unmarked and anonymous graves that were hastily dug on the battlefields where they fell. Some were transported home and buried in local cemeteries. A fraction of the Civil War dead were laid to rest at the newly established Arlington Cemetery.

Here, thousands of headstones mark the graves of Union soldiers, bearing the simple inscription "Unknown U.S. Soldier." Civilian dead, likewise, were interred at Arlington, including former slaves who had fled from the Confederacy and then perished behind Union lines. Larger and more elaborate monuments enshrine the burial sites of Union commanders such as Philip Sheridan, Philip Kearny, and seventy-nine other Union generals. As a testament to the Civil War's deadly devastation, 2,111 unknown Union dead received a place of honor in Arlington Cemetery in 1866.

The remains of several hundred Confederate dead, many of them prisoners who had died in local hospitals, also lay in graves scattered about the Arlington property. But, for its first thirty-five years as a national cemetery, the Confederate dead at Arlington received no formal recognition. Mourners who came to pay their respects to these deceased Southerners were turned away. By the close of the Spanish-American War in 1902, however, Northerners showed a new willingness to embrace the former rebels, especially since many had fought alongside Union men in the war against Spanish control of Cuba and the Philippines. As Americans celebrated a new era of patriotic reconciliation, they extended a place of honor to the ex-Confederates, both living and dead.

In 1901, four hundred Confederates were reinterred in a new Confederate section of Arlington Cemetery, their graves placed in a circle which, after 1914, had at its center a tall bronze memorial meant to symbolize the South at peace. By now, too, the cemetery included men and women who had perished in other American wars. At the close of the twentieth century, Arlington Cemetery contained the graves of more than 225,000 war veterans, two U.S. presidents, numerous men and women who served the military as medical personnel, and other noteworthy civilians.

Still, in neither life nor death did Robert E. Lee ever return to his former home. In the summer of 1865, with the war just concluded, he retreated to a friend's estate in the Virginia countryside. By the fall of that year, he had

General Irvin McDowell, serving as commander of the Union camp at Arlington, complied with Mary Lee's request to have some of her Arlington slaves sent to her. Two months later, McDowell (fifth man from the right) became the commander of the Union forces in the battle of First Bull Run.

accepted a position as President of Washington College in Lexington, Virginia. For the rest of his days, until his death in October 1870, Lee made his home at the college. He was buried in the Washington College Chapel.

In time, though, Lee's name and life would again be linked to the Arlington House. In 1882, Robert E. Lee's eldest son successfully sued the United States for the return of his family's property. But rather than take the land that was now covered with grave sites, Custis Lee allowed the government to retain the Arlington estate and old plantation home, in exchange for $150,000.

In 1925, the U.S. Congress agreed to transform the house, used for nearly sixty years as an office for the cemetery's superintendent, into a memorial for Robert E. Lee. With many Americans now willing to embrace General Lee as a brave and valiant commander, despite his Southern sympathies, the U.S. government saw in the former Lee home a fitting site for recalling Lee's life and work. The home was restored with furnishings that reflect the lifestyle which the Lees, once a prominent slaveowning family, would have enjoyed in the pre–Civil War period before Southern life was completely and irrevocably transformed.

ARLINGTON NATIONAL CEMETERY

Arlington, VA 22211
703-607-8052
www.arlingtoncemetery.org
NPS

On June 15, 1864, Secretary of War Edwin Stanton officially declared the Lee estate, along with two hundred acres of surrounding land, as a national military cemetery. In December 1863, a portion of these grounds was used for a model community for freed slaves that stayed in existence until 1890. Today, the Department of the Army administers the cemetery. Over 260,000 are buried here, including thousands of Civil War soldiers, both black and white, as well as 3,800 former slaves.

LEE CHAPEL, WASHINGTON AND LEE UNIVERSITY

Lexington, VA 24450
540-463-8768
www.leechapel.wlu.edu
NHL

The chapel was built in 1867 under the supervision of Robert E. Lee during his tenure as president of Washington College. After Lee's death in 1870, the school was renamed to honor both Lee as well as Washington. Lee and his family are buried beneath the building, which also reconstructs part of Lee's office at the school. A recumbent statue of Lee (below) by Edward Valentine is located at this chapel.

CULPEPPER NATIONAL CEMETERY

305 US Ave.
Culpepper, VA 22701
540-825-0027
www.cr.nps.gov/nr/travel/journey/cul.htm

The Culpepper National Cemetery was established in April 1867 to bury more than two thousand soldiers, particularly the Union dead from the battle of Cedar Mountain, fought on August 9, 1862. Union Quartermaster General Montgomery C. Meigs designed the superintendent's lodge, built in 1872. Since that time the cemetery has doubled in size to relieve pressure on Arlington National Cemetery. It now serves as a burial ground for veterans of all wars and their dependents.

GENERAL GRANT NATIONAL MEMORIAL (GRANT'S TOMB)

Riverside Drive and
    West 122 Street
New York, NY 10027
212-666-1640
www.nps.gov/gegr
NPS

After General Ulysses Grant died in 1885, about ninety thousand people from around the world sent more than $600,000 in a major public fund-raising effort to construct a tomb. Architect John Duncan completed the marble and granite structure in 1897. More than one million people attended the parade and dedication ceremony held that same year. General Grant and his wife, Julia Dent Grant, are buried here, in the largest mausoleum in the United States.

Chronology

February 1860

Abraham Lincoln gives a pivotal speech on slavery for the Republican party at the Cooper Union building in New York

May 1860

Lincoln is nominated as Republican Presidential candidate

November 1860

Lincoln is elected sixteenth President of the United States

December 1860

South Carolina passes an ordinance calling for secession from the United States

January 1861

Mississippi, Florida, Alabama, Georgia, and Louisiana adopt secession ordinances

February 1861

Texas secedes

Confederate States of America forms and ratifies a constitution

Jefferson Davis takes office as President of the Conferderate States of American in Montgomery, Alabama, the first capital of the Confederacy

March 1861

Abraham Lincoln is inaugurated President of the United States

April 1861

Fort Sumter in Charleston Harbor is fired upon by Confederate forces

The Union and Confederacy mobilize for war. Virginia, North Carolina, Tennessee, and Arkansas secede

Women meet in Cooper Union to organize the Women's Central Association of Relief, forerunner of the U.S. Sanitary Commission

May 1861

Confederate capital relocates to Richmond, Virginia

July 1861

First major military engagement occurs at Manassas, Virginia

Clara Barton begins nursing wounded soldiers in the U.S. Patent Office, Washington, D.C.

October 1861

Cherokee leader Stand Watie becomes a Confederate colonel

November 1861

Confederate diplomats James Mason and John Slidell are captured on their way to Europe and imprisoned at Fort Warren in Boston Harbor

December 1861

Fearing intervention from European powers, Lincoln releases Mason and Slidell from prison

March 1862

In the world's first battle between ironclad ships, the Union's *Monitor* and the Confederate's *Virginia* (formerly the *Merrimack*), duel to a draw near Norfolk, Virginia

The Confederates destroy the *Virginia* in May to keep it from falling into Union hands

800 Cherokees fight on the Confederate side in a battle at Pea Ridge, Arkansas

May 1862

Escaped slave Robert Smalls seizes a Confederate dispatch boat at Fort Sumter and delivers it to Union forces

June 1862

Robert E. Lee becomes supreme commander of Confederate forces in Virginia and eventually forces the retreat of Union forces that are under the command of Gen. George McClellan, who have reached the outskirts of Richmond

July 1862

Congress authorizes President Lincoln to enlist black troops

August 1862

Confederates are victorious at the Second Battle of Bull Run (Manassas)

September 1862

Lee invades Maryland; his campaign into the North is stopped at the battle of Antietam where wounded soldiers are attended to in the field by Clara Barton

President Lincoln issues a preliminary Emancipation Proclamation declaring slaves in the secession states to be free.

January 1863

The Emancipation Proclamation takes effect

May 1863

African-American troops battle unsuccessfully at Port Hudson, Louisiana, as part of the Union effort to control the Mississippi River

June 1863

Lee begins a campaign into Pennsylvania

July 1863

Union troops turn back the Confederates at Gettysburg, Pennsylvania

Grant captures Vicksburg, Mississippi, and Confederates surrender at Port Hudson, giving the Union control of the Mississippi

Colonel Robert Gould Shaw leads the 54th Massachusetts (Colored) regiment in an assault on Fort Wagner, South Carolina

Mobs riot in the streets of New York against new federal draft laws

Union and Confederate troops, including significant numbers of Native Americans on both sides, battle at Honey Springs, Oklahoma, in the largest Civil War battle in Indian Territory

September 1863

Confederate hopes in the west are renewed with victory at Chickamauga, Tennessee

November 1863

Lincoln delivers the Gettysburg Address

February 1864

Newly-constructed Andersonville prison in Georgia receives its first group of Union prisoners

March 1864

General Ulysses S. Grant assumes command of all Union armies

April 1864

Black Union soldiers are slaughtered in a Confederate assault on Fort Pillow, Tennessee

Grant suspends the prisoner exchange policy because of Confederates' refusal to exchange black prisoners of war

May 1864

In the Wilderness region and at Spotsylvania, Grant initiates an aggressive campaign against Lee's army in Virginia

June 1864

Abraham Lincoln is renominated Republican Presidential candidate

The siege of Petersburg, Virginia, begins with both Union and Confederate armies entrenched there for the next ten months

Robert E. Lee's former residence at Arlington becomes a U.S. cemetery

August 1864

George McClellan is nominated to be Lincoln's Democratic opponent

September 1864

General William T. Sherman captures Atlanta, Georgia

November 1864

Lincoln is reelected

Sherman begins his campaign through Georgia and the Carolinas

January 1865

Congress passes the Thirteenth Amendment to the Constitution, making Lincoln's Emancipation Proclamation the law of the entire land

March 1865

Lincoln is inaugurated for his second term as President; the reception is held at the U.S. Patent Office

The Confederates are unable to stop Sherman's onslaught in battle at Bentonville, North Carolina

April 1865

Lee surrenders to Grant at Appomattox Court House, Virginia

Jefferson Davis and family flee from Richmond

President Lincoln is assassinated by John Wilkes Booth

Further Reading

General Civil War History

Boritt, Gabor, ed. *War Comes Again: Comparative Vistas on the Civil War and World War II*. New York: Oxford University Press, 1995.

———. *Why the Civil War Came*. New York: Oxford University Press, 1996.

———. *Why the Confederacy Lost*. New York: Oxford University Press, 1992.

Bradford, Ned, ed. *Battles and Leaders of the Civil War*. 4 vols. 1883. Reprint, Edison, N. J.: Castle, 1985.

Catton, Bruce. *The American Heritage New History of the Civil War*. James McPherson, ed. New York: Viking, 1996.

Denney, Robert. *The Civil War Years*. New York: Sterling, 1992.

Eicher, David. *Mystic Chords of Memory: Civil War Battlefields and Historic Sites Recaptured*. Baton Rouge: Louisiana State University Press, 1998.

Faust, Patricia L., ed. *Historical Times Illustrated Encyclopedia of the Civil War*. New York: Harper, 1986.

Foote, Shelby. *The Civil War: A Narrative*. 3 vols. New York: Random House, 1958, 1963, 1974.

Horwitz, Tony. *Confederates in the Attic: Dispatches from the Unfinished Civil War*. New York: Vintage Books, 1999.

Katcher, Philip. *The Civil War Source Book*. New York: Facts on File, 1992.

Kennedy, Frances H., ed. *The Civil War Battlefield Guide*. Boston: Houghton Mifflin, 1990.

Linenthal, Edward. *Sacred Ground: Americans and Their Battlefields*. Urbana: University of Illinois Press, 1993.

McPherson, James, *Battle Cry of Freedom: The Civil War Era*. New York: Oxford University Press, 1988.

Miles, Jim. *Forged in Fire: A History and Tour Guide of the War in the East, From Manassas to Antietam, 1861–1862*. Nashville, Tenn.: Cumberland, 2000.

Muench, David. *Landscapes of Battle: The Civil War*. Jackson: University Press of Mississippi, 1988.

Stanchak, John. *The Visual Dictionary of the Civil War*. New York: Kindersley, 2000.

Symonds, Craig L. *A Battlefield Atlas of the Civil War*. 5th ed. Baltimore: Nautical and Aviator Publishing, 1988.

Ward, Geoffrey C., with Ric Burns and Ken Burns. *The Civil War*. New York: Knopf, 1990.

Wertz, Jay, and Edwin C. Bearss. *Smithsonian's Great Battles and Battlefields of the Civil War*. New York: Morrow, 1997.

Wiley, Bell Irvin. *The Life of Billy Yank: The Common Soldier of the Union*. Baton Rouge: Louisiana State University Press, 1984.

———. *The Life of Johnny Reb: The Common Soldier of the Confederacy*. Baton Rouge: Louisiana State University Press, 1984.

The Cooper Union Building

Donald, David. *Lincoln*. New York: Simon and Schuster, 1996.

Gienapp, William. *Abraham Lincoln and Civil War America*. New York: Oxford University Press, 2002.

Mayer, Henry. *All on Fire: William Lloyd Garrison and the Abolition of Slavery*. New York: St. Martin's Press, 1988.

Fort Sumter National Monument

Woodward, C. Vann, and Elisabeth Muhlenfeld, eds. *The Private Mary Chesnut: The Unpublished Civil War Diaries*. New York: Oxford University Press, 1984.

Current, Richard N. *Lincoln and the First Shot.* Philadelphia: Lippincott, 1963.

Klein, Maury. *Days of Defiance: Sumter, Secession, and the Coming of the Civil War.* New York: Random House, 1999.

The White House of the Confederacy

Cooper, William. *Jefferson Davis: American.* New York: Knopf, 2000.

Lankford, Nelson. *Richmond Burning: The Last Days of the Confederate Capital.* New York: Viking, 2002.

Van der Heuvel, Gerry. *Crowns of Thorns and Glory: Mary Todd Lincoln and Varina Howell Davis: The Two First Ladies of the Civil War.* New York: Dutton, 1988.

Manassas National Battlefield Park

Blackett, R. J .M., ed. *Thomas Morris Chester, Black Civil War Correspondent: His Dispatches from the Virginia Front.* Baton Rouge: Louisiana State University Press, 1989.

Harris, Brayton. *Blue and Grey in Black and White: The Newspapers in the American Civil War.* McLean, Va.: Brassey's, 1999.

Perry, James M. *A Bohemian Brigade: Civil War Correspondents—Mostly Rough, Sometimes Ready.* New York: Wiley, 2000.

Wallace, Mike. *Mickey Mouse History and Other Essays on American Memory.* Philadelphia: Temple University Press, 1996.

Zenzen, Joan M. *Battling for Manassas: The Fifty-Year Preservation Struggle at Manassas National Battlefield Park.* College Park: Pennsylvania State University Press, 1998.

National Museum of American Art and National Portrait Gallery

Alcott, Louisa May. *Hospital Sketches.* 1863. Reprint, Boston: Applewood, 1986.

Cummings, Kate. *Kate: The Journal of a Confederate Nurse.* Richard Barksdale Harwell, ed. Baton Rouge: Louisiana State University Press, 1998.

Oates, Stephen. *A Woman of Valor: Clara Barton and the Civil War.* New York: Free Press, 1994.

Staubing, Harold E. *In Hospital and Camp: The Civil War through the Eyes of its Doctors and Nurses.* Harrisburg, Pa.: Stackpole, 1993.

Taylor, Susie King. *Reminiscences of My Life in Camp with the 33rd U.S. Colored Troops.* New York: Wiener, 1988.

Wilber, C. Keith. *Civil War Medicine, 1861–1865.* Chatham N.J.: Chelsea House, 1999.

Tannehill Furnace

Edwards, William B. *Civil War Guns: The Complete Story of Federal and Confederate Small Arms: Design, Manufacture, Identification, Procurement, Issue, Employment, Effectiveness and Postwar Disposal.* Rev. ed. Austin, Tex.: Thomas, 1998.

Black, Robert C. *The Railroads of the Confederacy.* Chapel Hill: University of North Carolina Press, 1998.

Dew, Charles. *Ironmaker to the Confederacy: Joseph R. Anderson and the Tredegar Iron Works.* Richmond: Library of Virginia, 2000.

Port Hudson

Blatt, Martin H., Thomas J. Brown, and Donald Yacovone. *Hope and Glory: Essays on the Legacy of the 54th Massachusetts Regiment.* Amherst: University of Massachusetts Press, 2001.

Cornish, Dudley Taylor. *The Sable Arm: Black Troops in the Union Army, 1861–65.* Lawrence: University Press of Kansas, 1987.

Emilio, Luis F. *A Brave Black Regiment: The History of the Fifty-Fourth Regiment of Massachusetts Volunteer Infantry, 1863–65.* New York: Da Capo, 1995.

Glatthaar, Joseph. *Forged in Battle: The Civil War Alliance of Black Soldiers and White Officers.* New York: Free Press, 1990.

Higginson, Thomas Wentworth. *Army Life in a Black Regiment, and Other Writings.* New York: Penguin, 1997.

McPherson, James M. *The Negro's Civil War: How American Blacks Felt and Acted During the War for the Union.* New York: Ballantine, 1991.

Trudeau, Noah Andrew. *Like Men of War: Black Troops in the Civil War, 1862–65.* Boston: Little, Brown, 1998.

Gettysburg National Military Park

Bernstein, Iver. *The New York City Draft Riots.* New York: Oxford University Press, 1991.

Frassanito, William A. *Gettysburg: A Journey in Time.* New York: Scribner, 1975.

Grimsley, Mark, and Brooks D. Simpson. *Gettysburg: A Battlefield Guide.* Lincoln: University of Nebraska Press, 1999.

McPherson, James M. "Gettysburg, 1862." *American Heritage:* September 1999, pp. 49–53.

Shaara, Michael. *Killer Angels.* New York: Ballantine, 1974.

Stackpole, Edward J., and Wilbur S. Nye. *The Battle of Gettysburg: A Guided Tour.* Harrisburg, Penn.: Stackpole, 1960, 1963.

Honey Springs Battlefield

Hauptman, Laurence. *Between Two Fires: American Indians in the Civil War.* New York: Free Press, 1995.

Wallace, Anthony F. C. *The Long Bitter Trail: Andrew Jackson and the Indians.* New York: Hill and Wang, 1993.

White, Christine Schultz, and Benton R. White. *Now the Wolf Has Come: The Creek Nation in the Civil War.* College Station: Texas A & M University Press, 1996.

Andersonville National Historic Site

Denney, Robert E. *Civil War Prisons and Escapes: A Day-by-Day Chronicle.* New York: Sterling Publishing Co., 1993.

Marvel, William. *Andersonville: The Last Depot.* Chapel Hill: University of North Carolina Press, 1994.

Ripple, Ezra Hoyt. *Dancing Along the Deadline: The Andersonville Memoir of a Prisoner of the Confederacy.* Novato, Cal.: Presidio, 1996.

Appomattox Court House National Historical Park

Bradley, Mark. *This Astounding Close.* Chapel Hill: University of North Carolina Press, 2000.

Marvel, William. *A Place Called Appomattox.* Chapel Hill: University of North Carolina Press, 2000.

Smith, Gene. "The Last Rebel Ground." *American Heritage:* April 1999, pp. 83–92.

Arlington House, The Robert E. Lee Memorial

Bigler, Philip. *In Honored Glory: Arlington National Cemetery, The Final Post.* Arlington, Va.: Vandamere, 1999.

Blight, David. *Race and Reunion.* Cambridge, Mass.: Harvard University Press, 2000.

Fellman, Michael. *The Making of Robert E. Lee.* New York: Random House, 2000.

Reef, Catherine. *Arlington National Cemetery.* Parsippany, N. J. Silver Burdett Ginn, 1991.

Thomas, Emory. *Robert E. Lee: A Biography.* New York: Norton, 1995.

Index

References to illustrations and their captions are in *italic*. References to maps are indicated by *m*.

Abolitionists, and raid on Harpers Ferry, 14–15

African Americans: contributions of during Civil War, 13; and Fort Sumter, 32; and Medals of Honor, 82; nurses and nursing, 60; and Port Hudson, 71–81; as prisoners of war, 101, 109; and war correspondents, 51. *See also* Biggs, Basil; Fifty-fourth Massachusetts Regiment; Louisiana Native Guards

Agrarian way of life, 66

Alabama. *See* Alabama State Capitol; Tannehill Furnace

Alabama State Capitol, 43, 45

Alexander, John, 69

Alexander, Peter, 49, 53

Ambulance corps, *59*

American history, and Civil War, 12, 20

American Red Cross, 61, 62

Anderson, Robert, 25, 27, 28, 29, 33

Andersonville National Historic Site (Ga.), 106–14, *107m*, 136

Andrew, John, 76

Antietam National Battlefield (Md.), 95

Appomattox Court House National Historical Park (Va.), 13, 115–23, *116m*, 136

Architecture: of Arlington House, 125; of Cooper Union Building, 16, *17*; of Old Patent Office, 57, 60

Arkansas. *See* Pea Ridge National Military Park

Arlington House (Robert E. Lee Memorial) (Va.), 124–30, *125m*, 136

Arlington National Cemetery (Va.), 13, 128–29, 131

Armstrong Academy Site (Okla.), 98, 105

Army. *See* Department of the Army; Union Army

Atwater, Dorance, 106–07, 111–12

Banks, Nathaniel, 73, 75, 79, 80

Barton, Clara, 56, 58–59, 61, 62, 111–12, 114

Battery Wagner (S.C.), 28

Battlefields, and Civil War landscape, 12–13. *See also* Honey Springs Battlefield; Manassas National Battlefield Park

Beauregard, Pierre, 26, 29, *32*, 47

Beauvoir House (Miss.), 45

Beecher, Henry Ward, 15

Belle Isle Jail (Va.), 106, *108*

Benjamin, Judah, 37

Bennett Place State Historic Site (N.C.), 123

Bentonville Battlefield (N.C.), 62

Biggs, Basil, 85–86, 91, 93

Blockade, naval, 69

Blunt, James, 100

Booth, John Wilkes, 24

Brady, Matthew, *14*, 50

Brockenbrough, John, 35

Brown, John, 14–15

Bullets, 68

Bull Run. *See* Manassas National Battlefield Park

Butler, Benjamin, 74

Cailloux, André, 71, 75, 77, 79, 80, 81

Cairo, USS (ship), 95

Carney, William, 82

Carter, Landon, Jr., 50

Casualty rates, and Civil War, 68, 76, 79–80, 85, 87, 95, 128

Cedar Mountain, Battle of (1862), 131

Cemetery, at Andersonville prison, *112*. *See also* Arlington National Cemetery; Culpepper National Cemetery; Gettysburg National Cemetery

Censorship, of newspapers, 48–49

Chamberlain, Joshua, 120

Charleston, South Carolina, *26m*. *See also* Fort Sumter

Charleston Courier, 49

Cherokee Nation, 96–97, 97–98, 100, 102–04, 105

Chester, Thomas Morris, 51, 78

Chesnut, Mary, 31, 32–33, 37, 38–39

Chicago Tribune, 50

Choctaw Indians, 97, 98, 101, 105

Civil War: causes of, 20; chronology of events, 132–33; end of, 78, 115; and Fort Sumter, 31; further readings on, 134; as pivotal event in American history, 12; preservation of historic sites, 54. *See also* African Americans; Battlefields; casualty rates; Confederate States of America; Native Americans

Clara Barton National Historic Site (Md.), 62

Clerisseau, Louis, 45

Collins, William "Mosby," 110

Confederate Memorial Literary Society, 44

Confederate States of America: capitol of, 43; Constitution, 40–41; formation of government, 27; and Gettysburg National Military Park, 93–94; and Native Americans, 98; secession and Fort Sumter, 31; and surrender at Appomattox, 119–20, 121. *See also* South

Conscription laws, 23

Constitution, Confederate, 40–41

Cooper, Douglas H., 100, 101

Cooper, Peter, 15–16

Cooper Union Building (N.Y.), 13, 14–19, 15*m*, 21–23, 134

"Corps d'Afrique,' 74

Cotton, and economy of South, 65–66, 69, 70

"Cradle of the Confederacy," 43

Crawford, Samuel Wylie, 26

Creek Nation, 97, 98

Crenshaw, Lewis, 35

Crenshaw Woolen Mills (Va.), 70

Crowder, John, 75, 77, 80

Culpepper National Cemetery (Va.), 131

Custis, George Washington Parke, 124, 125, 126

Custis, John Parke, 125

Davis, Jefferson, *34*, 35, 36, 43, 45, 84, 118

Davis, Varina Howell, 36–39, 42

DeLeon, Thomas, 37

Department of the Army, 131

Dix, Dorothea, 59

Doctors, 58. *See also* Hospitals

Dorsey, Sarah, 45

Doubleday, Abner, 25, 30

Douglas, Stephen, 15, 18

Douglass, Frederick, 32, 51, 74, 76

Draft riots (New York City), 23

Dred Scott decision, 14

Duncan, John, 131

Dunlap, Myron, 122–23

Economy: and causes of Civil War, 20; and industry in South, 67, 69. *See also* Cotton; Railroads

Education: and Cooper Union Building, 19, 23; of Southern women, 36

Eisenhower National Historic Site (Pa.), 95

Elliot, William P., 60

Emancipation Proclamation (1863), 74, 75, 95

Engineering, and Cooper Union Building, 16, *17*. *See also* Architecture

Exchanges, of prisoners of war, 109, 114

Factories, 64, 67. *See also* Economy; Textile industry; Weapons

Faulkner, William, *83*

Fifty-fourth Massachusetts Regiment, 28, 76, 77, 82

Florida. *See* Fort Pickens

Fontaine, Felix Gregory de, 49

Food shortages, at Confederate prison, 108–09, 110

Ford's Theater National Historic Site (Wash., D.C.), 24

Forrest, Nathan Bedford, 82

Fort Davis (Okla.), 105

Fort Gibson (Okla.), 99, 100, 105

Fort Moultrie (S.C.), 27, 33

Fort Pickens (Fla.), 30, 33

Fort Pillow Historic Park (Tenn.), 82

Fort Sumter (S.C.), 13, 25–33, 26*m*, 134

Fort Wagner (S.C.), 76, 77

Fort Warren (Mass.), 113

"Free labor," 20

French, Daniel Chester, 24

General Grant National Memorial (Grant's Tomb) (N.Y.), 131

Georgia, 107*m*. *See also* Andersonville National Historic Site

Gettysburg Address (Lincoln 1863), 90, 92, 93

Gettysburg Battlefield Historic District (PA), 95

Gettysburg National Cemetery (PA), 90, 95

Gettysburg National Military Park (PA), 13, 54, 84*m*, 135–36

Glory (movie 1989), 76

Gordon, John, 118, 120

Gorgas, Josiah, 67

Grant, Julia Dent, 123, 131

Grant, Ulysses S., *117*: and Grant's Tomb, 131; home in Missouri, 123; and siege of Vicksburg, 72–73, 80–81, 83, 91, 95; and surrender at Appomattox, 115, 118–20

Great Britain, 69, 113

Great Hall. *See* Cooper Union Building

Greek Revival architectural style, 57, 60, 125

Greeley, Horace, 46, 55

Greeley House (N.Y.), 55

Gulf Islands National Seashore, 32

Guns, rifled, 68

Hadfield, George, 125

Hammond, James Henry, 65

Harper, John, 62

Harpers Ferry (Va.), 14–15

Harper's Weekly, 55

Henry, Judith Carter, 50

Hillman, Daniel, 64, 67

Hillyer, George, 88

Hilton Head, South Carolina, *19*

Historic preservation, 54, 94

Holt, Barachias, 45

Homer, Winslow, 55

Honey Springs Battlefield (Okla.), 13, 96–104, 97*m*, 136

Hospitals, 57–61, 107, 110. *See also* Doctors; Nurses and nursing

Illinois. *See* Lincoln Home National Historic Site

Indian Home Guard, 100

Indian Territory (Okla.), 97, 98, 100, 104

Industry, 64–65, 66. *See also* Economy; Textile industry; Weapons

Iron and Steel Museum (Ala.), 67, 69

Jackson, Thomas J. (Stonewall), 47, 52, 55

Jefferson, Thomas, 45

John Ross House (Ga.), 105

Johnston, Joseph, 47, 81, 118

Journalists, and Manassas Battleground, 13, 48–53, 55. *See also* Newspapers

Kansas, Native Americans and Kansas Home Guards, 98

Kansas Colored Volunteers, 101

Kearney, Philip, 128

Landscape: Gettysburg and Confederate point of view, 93–94; impact of Civil War on, 12; preservation of Civil War sites, 54; and "sense of place," 141

Lee, Agnes, *127*

Lee, Custis, 130

Lee, Mary Custis, 124–25, 126, 127, 128

Lee, Mildred, *127*

Lee, Robert E.: and Arlington House, 124–30; and Battle of Gettysburg, 83–85, 86–87, 89, 91, 95; and Battle of Manassas, 53, 55; and Confederate campaign in Pennsylvania, 83; as president of Washington College, 131; statue of in Virginia, 94; and surrender at Appomattox, 115, *117*, 118–20, 121, *122*

Lee Chapel, Washington and Lee University (Va.), 131

Leslie's Illustrated Newspaper, 96

Liberia, and recolonization of African Americans, 51

Lincoln, Abraham, *14*: assassination of, 24; and Battle of Manassas, 47; and debates with Douglas, 15; election of as president, 26; and family home in Illinois, 24; and Fort Sumter, 29, 31, 32; and Gettysburg Address, 90, 92, 93; response of to letter from John Ross, *99* and Richmond, Virginia, 44; and speech at Cooper Union Building, 14, 17–19, 22; and Vicksburg, Mississippi, 81. *See also* Lincoln Memorial

Lincoln, Robert, 19

Lincoln Home National Historic Site (Ill.), 24

Lincoln Memorial (Wash., D.C.), 24

Livermore, Mary Ashton, 31

London Times, 49

Longstreet, James, 83, 86–87, 89

Louisiana, African Americans and postwar politics, 51. *See also* New Orleans; Port Hudson

Louisiana Native Guards, 71, 73–74, 75, 79

Lowell National Historical Park (Mass.), 70

Maine. *See* Winslow Homer Studio, 55

Manassas National Battlefield Park (Va.), 13, 46–55, 48m, 135

Manufacturing, 64–65. *See also* Economy; Textile industry; Weapons

Maryland. *See* Clara Barton National Historic Site

Mason, James, 113

Massachusetts. *See* Fort Warren; Lowell National Historical Park; Saugus Iron Works National Historic Site

McDowell, Irvin, 47, 49, 50, 127, *129*

McIntosh family (Creek), 98

McLean, Wilmer, 116–17, 119, 120, 122

Meade, George, 85

Medal of Honor, 82

Meigs, Montgomery, 128, 131

Merrimack (ship), 66–67

Metropolitan District Commission (Mass.), 113

Mills, Robert, 35, 36, 57, 60

Minie, Claude E., 68

Mississippi. *See also* Beauvoir House; Vicksburg

Mississippi River: battle for control of, 72–73, 81, 95; and Trail of Tears route, 105. *See also* Vicksburg

Missouri, 105. *See also* Trail of Tears State Park Archaeological Site; Ulysses S. Grant National Historic Site

Monitor (ship), 66–67

Montgomery, Alabama, 43

Monuments, Civil War, 93–94, 114, *128*. *See also* General Grant National Memorial

Morris Island (S.C.), 28

Museum of the Confederacy (Va.), 34–39, 42, 44

National Historic Preservation Act of 1966, 141

National Museum of American Art and National Portrait Gallery (Wash., D.C.), 56–62, 57m, 135

National Park Service, 33, 54, 94, 105, 112, 114, 123, 141

National Park System, 141

National Prisoner of War Museum (Ga.), *110*

National Register of Historic Places, 141

National Register Information System (NRIS), 141

Native Americans, and Honey Springs Battlefield, 13, 96–104

Naval warfare, 67, 69

New Castle Historical Society (N.Y.), 55

New Orleans, 72, 80

Newspapers, 19, 48–49. *See also* journalists

New York. *See* Cooper Union Building; General Grant National Memorial; Greeley House

New York City, and Cooper Union Building, 15m

New York Herald, 51

New York Times, 50, 80, 109

New York Tribune, 46, 47, 52, 55, 76

North Carolina, *106*. *See also* Bennett Place State Historic Site; Bentonville Battlefield

Nurses and nursing, 56–57, 58–61. *See also* Hospitals

Oklahoma. *See* Fort Gibson; Honey Springs Battlefield

Oklahoma Historical Society, 104

Old Patent Office Building (Wash., D.C.), 56–62

Old Slater Mill (R.I.), 70

O'Neill, James, *96*

Opothleyahola, Chief (Creek), 98

Ordnance Bureau (Confederate), 67

O'Sullivan, Timothy, *89*

Parker, Ely S., 97

Pea Ridge National Military Park (Ark.), 105

Pennsylvania, Confederate campaign in, 84. *See also* Gettysburg National Cemetery; Gettysburg National Military Park

Peterson, Frederick A., 16, 18

Philadelphia Press, 51, 78

Pickett, George, 83, 85, 89

Pike, Albert, 98

Politics: and causes of Civil War, 20; postwar Louisiana and African Americans, 51

Pope, John, 53, 55

"Popular sovereignty," 18

Port Hudson (La.), 13, 71–91, 72m, 135

Presidents, and Arlington National Cemetery, 129. *See also* Lincoln, Abraham

Prisons and prisoners of war, 75, 101, 106–14. *See also* African Americans; Andersonville National Historic Site; Exchanges
Pryor, J. P., 53

Railroads, 47, 50, 65, 67
Raine, Charles, 118
Republican party, 14, 15, 18, 19, 22
Republic Steel Corporation, 69
Revisionist history, 20
Rhode Island. *See* Old Slater Mill
Richmond, Virginia, 34, 35–36, 42, 44, 51, 118
Richmond National Battlefield Park (Va.), 82
Robinson, James, 50
Ross, John, 97–98, *99*, 101, 105
Russell, William Howard, 49, 53

St. Gaudens, Augustus, 76
St. Mary's Church (Va.), 62
Sanders, William L., 67
Saunders, William, 90
Savannah Republican, 49, 53
Scientific American, 17
Scott, Dred, 14
Secession, of Southern states, 26–27, 31
Seminole Indians, 98
Seneca Indians, 97
"Sense of place," 141
Seward, William, 15, 29, 30
Shaw, Robert Gould, 76, 82
Shebangs, 107
Sheridan, Philip, 104, 128
Sherman, William T., 62, 104, 110, 118, 123
Slater, Samuel, 70
slavery, *19, 38*: and Arlington House, 125–26; causes of Civil War, 20; Confederate Constitution, 40–41; Dred Scott decision, 14; and Emancipation, 74–75; and industry in South, 64, 67; and Lincoln's speech at Cooper Union, 17, 22; in Richmond, Virginia, 38–39

Slidell, John, 113
Smalls, Robert, 33
Smith, Joshua B., 82
Smithsonian Institution, 62
South: and agrarian way of life, 66; and education of women, 36; location of Tannehill Furnace, 64m; and monuments to Civil War participants, 93–94; and plantation residences, 125–26 *See also* Confederate States of America
South Carolina, 27. *See also* Charleston; Fort Moultrie; Fort Sumter; Fort Wagner; Hilton Head; Morris Island
Spanish-American War, 33, 128
Stanton, Edwin, 109, 131
State's rights, 20
Stephens, Alexander, 113, 114
Supreme Court, 14
Surrender, at Appomattox, 119–20, 121

Tannehill, Ninion, 64
Tannehill Furnace (Tannehill Ironworks Historical State Park) (Ala.), 63–69, 64m, 135
Taylor, Susie King, 60
Teaching with Historic Places program (TwHP), 141
Telegraph, 48, 49, 50
Tennessee. *See* Fort Pillow Historic Park
Textile industry, 65, 69, 70
Town, Ithiel, 60
"Trail of Tears," 97, 105
Trail of Tears State Park Archaeological Site (Missouri), 105
Tredegar Iron Works (Va.), 64, 66, 70

Ulysses S. Grant National Historic Site (Mo.), 123
Union Army, and African Americans, 75
U.S. Army Corps of Engineers, 28
U.S. Sanitary Commission, 21, 59, 61
University of Alabama, 69

Vicksburg, Mississippi, *38*, 72–73, 80, 83, *8*, 91, 95
Vicksburg National Military Park (MS), 95
Virginia, 57m. *See also* Appomattox Court House National Historical Park; Arlington House; Lee Chapel; Manassas National Battlefield Park; Richmond; Tredegar Iron Works; White House of the Confederacy (Museum of the Confederacy)
Virginia State Capitol, 45

Walt Disney Company, 54
Walter, Thomas U., 57, 60
Warren, Fitz Henry, 46
War veterans, and Arlington National Cemetery, 129
Washington, DC, 57. *See also* Old Patent Office
Washington, George, 125
Washington College (Va.), 129, 131
Water supply, at Confederate prison, 108
Watie, Stand, 96, 97, 98–99, 102, 103
Weapons, and manufacturing, 63–69
White House of the Confederacy (Museum of the Confederacy) (Va.), 34–39, 35m, 42, 44, 135
Whitman, Walt, 60–61
Wilkes, Charles, 113
Winslow Homer Studio (Maine), 55
Wirz, Henrich, 111, 114
Woman's Central Association of Relief (WCAR), 19, 21, 23
Women: contributions of to Civil War effort, 19, 21, 23; education of Southern, 36; service in hospitals, 59, 60. *See also* Nurses and nursing

Young Men's Central Republican Union (NY), 15

Zouave regiments, 52

The National Register of Historic Places, National Park Service

The National Register of Historic Places is the official U.S. list of historic places worthy of preservation. Authorized under the National Historic Preservation Act of 1966, the National Register is part of a national program to coordinate and support public and private efforts to identify, evaluate, and protect America's historic and archeological resources. The National Register is administered by the National Park Service, which is part of the U.S. Department of the Interior.

Properties listed in the National Register include districts, sites, buildings, structures, and objects that are significant in U.S. history, architecture, archaeology, engineering, and culture. Places range from ancient Indian pueblos, to homes of writers or philanthropists, to bridges, to commercial districts. Among the tens of thousands of listings are: all historic areas in the National Park System; National Historic Landmarks; and properties nominated for their significance to communities, states, or the nation. The public can find information about these places on the web from the National Register Information System (NRIS) or request copies of documentation files.

For more information about the National Register of Historic Places, visit our Web site at www.cr.nps.gov/nr; phone 202-354-2213; fax 202-371-2229; e-mail nr_info@nps.gov; or write National Register of Historic Places, National Park Service, 1849 C Street, NW, Washington, DC 20240.

Teaching with Historic Places

The Teaching with Historic Places program (TwHP) uses places listed in the National Register to enrich and enliven the study of history, social studies, geography and other subjects. Historic places have the power to make us more aware of our connection to the people and events that preceded us. It is possible to experience that "sense of place" whether or not site visits are possible. By actively investigating places and documentation about them, students can develop enthusiasm and curiosity while they enjoy a historian's sense of discovery and learn critical skills.

A series of lessons based on places around the country forms the cornerstone of the TwHP program. It includes Revolutionary and Civil War battlefields, presidential homes, churches that hosted Civil Rights meetings, places where women made history, and much more. Each lesson plan includes an activity that leads students to research the history and historic places in their own communities. TwHP lessons are free and available online, where they are indexed by state, historic theme, time period, and the National Standards for History.

For more information about the award-winning TwHP program or to acquire the lesson plans, visit the TwHP Web site at www.cr.nps.gov/nr/twhp; phone 202-354-2213; fax 202-371-2229; e-mail nr_twhp@nps.gov; or write Teaching with Historic Places, National Register of Historic Places, National Park Service, 1849 C Street, NW, Washington, DC 20240.

Acknowledgments

Those who best know and appreciate the kinds of historic sites discussed in this book are the curators, historians, and park guides, and interpreters, who devote their energy to interpreting historic places. I am grateful to all of those experts, who provided me with essential information and assistance, especially Beth Boland and Carol Shull of the National Register of Historic Places and Alexis Abernathy, historian of the National Conference of State Historic Preservation Officers. Thanks, too, to Brion Fitzgerald and Kathy Harrison for their contributions to the Gettysburg chapter, and to Dean Herrin for clueing me in to the Tannehill Furnace. Denise Meringolo offered outstanding long-distance support, keeping me fully up-to-date on the Civil War, while I lived for a year in Prague. I also extend my gratitude to several Boston University graduate students—Cheryl Boots, Jennifer Green, Scott Hovey, and Bill Leeman—who lent their assistance at several critical junctures in the preparation of this manuscript. As with most things in my life, I am indebted to my husband, Louis Hutchins, who has shared his own insights as a National Park Service historian with me, and has given me a new appreciation for the significance of historic places.

Gilder Lehrman Institute of American History

The Gilder Lehrman Institute of American History promotes the study and love of American history. It organizes seminars and enrichment programs for teachers and National Park Service educators; creates history-centered high schools nationwide; supports and produces publications and traveling exhibitions for students and the general public; sponsors lectures by historians; develops electronic media projects, including the Institute's website; establishes research centers at universities and libraries; and grants and oversees fellowships for scholars to work in the Gilder Lehrman Collection and in other archives of American history. The Gilder Lehrman Institute may be contacted at:

19 W. 44th Street, Suite 500
New York, NY 10036-5902
646-366-9666
fax 646-366-9669
http://www.gilderlehrman.org

Oxford University Press would especially like to thank Gilder Lehrman Institute of American History for the following images: The Gilder Lehrman Collection, courtesy of The Gilder Lehrman Institute of American History, New York: 3, 7 (bottom), 19, 25 (top), 27, 29, 34 (top), 37 (top), 39, 40, 46, 55 (bottom left), 58 (top, bottom), 59, 61 (bottom), 65, 66, 73, 74, 81, 87, 89, 90, 99, 106, 109, 111, 115 (top), 120, 122, 124 (top, bottom)

Picture and Text Credits

Pictures Courtesy of Alabama Historic Ironworks Commission: 63, 67; Courtesy of Andersonville National Historic Site: 110, 112 (top); Courtesy of Appomattox Court House National Historical Park: 118; Archives and Manuscripts Division of the Oklahoma Historical Society: 96 (top); Courtesy of Arlington House, The Robert E. Lee Memorial (National Park Service): 126; Courtesy of Arlington National Cemetery Website *http://www.arlingtoncemetery.com*: 128, 131 (top); Courtesy Beauvoir: 45; Courtesy of Bennett Place, Photography by Ellis Williamson: 123; Courtesy of Boston Harbor Islands National Park Area. Photography by John Nove: 114; Courtesy of Chief John Ross House Assoc.: 105; Courtesy of choctawnation.com: 98; Courtesy of CivilWarAlbum.com: 100; Courtesy of The Cooper Union for the Advancement of Science and Art: 16, 18; Courtesy of Fort Pillow Historic Park: 82; John Bigelow Taylor, NYC. Feinmore Art Museum, Cooperstown, New York: 30; Courtesy of Fort Sumter National Monument: 28, 33; From the Collection of Gilcrease Museum, Tulsa: 102; Library of Congress, Prints and Photographs Division: NYTWS-Education Colleges-Cooper Union: 7 (top), 14 (bottom), 21; LC-USZ62-5803: 14 (top); LC-HAER-NY-31-NEYO: 17; [25] (bottom); LC-USZ62-15632: 32; LC-USZ62-23306: 35 (bottom); LC-USZC4-602: 42; LC-USZ62-6932: 44; LC-B8171-313; 47; LC-USZ62-111072: 49; LC-USZC4-611: 7 (middle), 52; LC-USZ62-92528: 56 (top); [Old Patent Office] (bottom); HABS-DC-WASH-503: 60; LC-BH82-137: 61 (top); LC-USZ62-6876: 62 (top); LC-AP2.H32: 71; LC-USZC4-507: 76; LC-USZ62-36202: 79; LC-USZ62-549: 83; LC-USZ62-31277: 86; LC-B8184-10454: 92; LC-USZ62-31294: 96 (bottom); LC-USZ62-26668: 108; LC-B817-7292: 115 (bottom); LC-USZ62-40854: 117; LC-USZ62-2480: 119; LC-B8184-4099: 129; Courtesy of the Lincoln Home National Historic Site: 24; Courtesy of Louisiana Office of Tourism: 75; Museum of the City of New York: 23; The Museum of the Confederacy Richmond, Virginia: 34 (bottom); The Museum of the Confederacy, Richmond, Virginia, Photography by Katherine Wetzel: 36, 37 (bottom), 127; National Archives 64-CN-9092: ii; Courtesy of National Park Service: 50, 54, 70, 85, 95 (top left); Collection of The New-York Historical Society: 112 (bottom); Courtesy of North Carolina Historic Sites: 62 (bottom); Courtesy of Old Court House Museum: 38; Courtesy of Alexis Siroc: 94, 95 (top); Courtesy of Jim Strongin (cover); Special Collections, University of Virginia: 53; Courtesy of Vicksburg National Military Park: 95 (middle); Courtesy of Washington and Lee University: 131 (bottom); Courtesy of Charles H. Willauer: 55 (bottom right)

Text p. 22: Philip Van Doren Stern, ed. *The Writings of Abraham Lincoln,* (New York: Modern Library, 1999), 588–91.

p. 40–41: Full text of the Constitution of the Confederate States of America can be found at *http://www.constitution.org/csa/csa_cons.htm.*

p. 78: RJM. Blackett, ed. *Thomas Morris Chester, Black Civil War Correspondent,* (Baton Rouge: Louisiana State University Press, 1989), 288–91.

p. 88: George Hillyer, letter, in *The Southern Banner,* July 29, 1863.

p. 92: Roy P. Basler, ed., *The Collected Works of Abraham Lincoln* Vol. 7 (New Brunswick, N.J.: Rutgers University Press, 1953–1955), 22.

p. 103: Stand Watie, letter to Governor of Creek Nation, in *The War of the Rebellion Official Records of the Union and Confederate Armies,* Ser. I., Volume 23, part 2, 1105–1106.

p. 121: Appomattox surrender document in *The War of the Rebellion: Official Records of the Union and Confederate Armies,* Ser. I., Vol. 46, part 3, 685–86.

Nina Silber is an associate professor of history at Boston University where she specializes in the Civil War era. Her books include *The Romance of Reunion: Northerners and the South, 1865-1900*; *Yankee Correspondence: Civil War Letters Between New England Soldiers and the Homefront*; and *Divided Houses: Gender and the Civil War*. She has also consulted on numerous public history projects and is currently on the Museum Advisory Board for the Gettysburg National Battlefield Museum Foundation. She is now completing a book on Northern women and the Civil War.

James Oliver Horton is the Benjamin Banneker Professor of American Studies and History at George Washington University and director of the George Washington University Center for Public History and Public Culture. Horton has been honored with many awards for excellence in scholarship and teaching, as well as an appointment by President Clinton to serve on the Abraham Lincoln Bicentennial Commission. He has served as historical expert for First Lady Hillary Rodham Clinton on the White House Millennium Council; acting chair of the National Park System Advisory Board; Senior Advisor on Historical Interpretation and Public Education for the Director of the National Park Service; and historical advisor to museums throughout the world. In addition to consulting on film and video productions, he has himself been the subject of an episode in The History Channel series "Great Minds in American History." His numerous books include *Free People of Color: Inside the African American Community*, *The History of the African American People* (co-edited with Lois E. Horton), and *In Hope of Liberty: Culture, Protest, and Community Among Northern Free Blacks, 1700–1860* (coauthored with Lois E. Horton). In 2004, Horton will assume the presidency of the Organization of American Historians.